PURPOSEFUL
DISCIPLESHIP

Pacer Hepperly

ISBN 979-8-9987709-1-3 (paperback)
ISBN 979-8-9987709-0-6 (hardcover)
ISBN 979-8-9987709-2-0 (digital)

Printed in the United States of America

"Spiritual growth happens intentionally, not automatically. My friend, Pacer Hepperly, has developed a powerful discipleship tool that will empower you to take responsibility for your spiritual growth, no matter where you find yourself in your faith journey."

John Bevere
Best-selling Author and Minister
Co-founder of Messenger International & MessengerX

"After pastoring for more than 40 years, I've always been haunted when the question was posed to me, 'What does your church's discipleship process look like?' I would find myself sidestepping the question because I knew we did not have an effective tool. Now I have an answer and that answer is a good one. *PURPOSEFUL DISCIPLESHIP*. It gets the entire church on the road to making disciples in an effective and highly relational wineskin. Pacer Hepperly has equipped the church with a tool that satisfies our Savior's challenge to go and make disciples in a time when the world is crying out for someone to show them the way."

Rev. JP Wilson
Pastor, Summit Church

Contents

INTRODUCTION

Congratulations on your interest in discipleship and your investment in this book. In the pages ahead, you will be encouraged to go deeper in your walk with Jesus while building meaningful relationships with others.

Purposeful Discipleship is a tool. It will guide you through foundational Biblical topics and stimulate thought and discussion in small group settings.

We understand that Jesus didn't mass-produce disciples using a one size fits all approach. So we have designed this book to afford greater flexibility and allow individuals to learn foundational truths at their own pace.

It is my heart's desire to see believers in Christ develop to their fullest potential. I hope you will find this book a good resource in helping facilitate this process.

Thank you,
Pacer

GETTING STARTED

An essential part of discipleship is discovering and persistently following a model that works for you. These instructional steps listed below are proven in theory and practice. They have been tested for more than a decade.

Step 1: You Have What It Takes

Leadership isn't as complicated as some may think. It only requires someone who is willing to follow and then lead. I'm sure Peter didn't know he had what it took when Jesus called him to follow and then go out and make disciples.

Step 2: Leading Others

Whether you view yourself as a leader or not, others need you to lead them in discipleship. Resources in this book will help you guide others to spiritual maturity

Step 3: Selecting the Right People

Identifying the right people to disciple is an important step and should begin with prayer. Ask the Lord to show you whom to invite into your discipleship group. The next step is an interview. You want to make sure each candidate is committed to this incredible journey.

Paul instructed Timothy on how to select potential candidates in 2 Timothy 2:2 (NLT)

"You have heard me teach things that have been confirmed by many reliable witnesses. Now teach these truths to other **trustworthy people who will be able to pass them on to others."**

Step 4: Setting a Date

Establish a time and day that works for you, and then stick to it. During the interview process, share the meeting's time, date, and location with each candidate to ensure total commitment. Changing meeting times to accommodate schedules has proven to be unproductive.

Step 5: Coming Prepared

Each week, all participants should come to the meeting prepared to share their memory verse and answers to chapter questions. If you are leading multiple participants, allow everyone to comment on each question before moving on to the next.

Step 6: Stay on Task

Keeping a group on task can be like herding cats. You want meaningful discussions related to the topic, but you must be able to reel it in when needed. Always allow the Holy Spirit to move throughout the conversations because this will be your most effective time. Make sure that quieter people have a chance to share in the discussions.

Step 7: Finish Strong

This book has 26 chapters designed to provide one year of discipleship training. To thoroughly discuss the assigned Bible study, most chapters require two one hour sessions. Some chapters can be completed in one session, allowing you to finish earlier.

After the book's completion, celebrate! Organize a commissioning ceremony involving spouses, friends, and family. You may want to hold the celebration in a home, restaurant, or during a church service. Regardless of location, as the leader, you will present a completion certificate and pray over the individual and his or her family.

Let's get started.

OUR MISSION

CHAPTER 1: OUR MISSION

Bible Study Verses: John 17
Memory Verse: Matthew 28:19

> Go therefore and make disciples of all nations, baptizing them in the name of the Father and of the Son and of the Holy Spirit. (Matthew 28:19 ESV)

Background

Jesus has been resurrected from the grave and revealed Himself to the disciples. He tells them to meet Him in Galilee for final instructions before His ascension. This is what has been referenced as the *Great Commission* and is essentially the mission statement of the Church.

Memory Verse Questions

1. Why is there such a great emphasis placed on this particular scripture?

   _____

   _____

   _____

2. How can we apply the word "go" to our discipleship training?

   _____

   _____

   _____

3. How could you see "all nations" being impacted through discipleship?

   _____

   _____

   _____

Bible Study Questions: John 17

Jesus, in His prayer to the Father, makes a statement in verse 4 that His work is complete. This work that Jesus was referencing is paramount in your journey to discipleship.

"There is no higher calling or greater privilege known to man than being involved in helping fulfill the Great Commission."

—Bill Bright—

1. What is the general setting of John 17?

    _____

    _____

    _____

    _____

    _____

2. Jesus prays for two groups of people. Identify the two groups.

    _____

    _____

    _____

    _____

    _____

3. What was the completed work Jesus was referring to in verse 4?

    _____

    _____

    _____

    _____

    _____

4. According to verse 8, how did the disciples respond to the words Jesus gave them? How are we to respond?

_____

_____

_____

_____

_____

5. What is the common theme Jesus prays for in verse 11 and verse 21?

_____

_____

_____

_____

_____

6. What does Psalm 133 say about unity in your own words?

_____

_____

_____

_____

_____

Words from the Author:

After thirty years of being a Christian, I've estimated hearing over 1,300 sermons, not including the numerous Sunday school classes and life groups I've attended. Over the years, I've delivered approximately six hundred sermons and taught many classes as a senior pastor. I've heard references to discipleship in sermons and class studies, but not as frequently as one might think.

Several years ago, I was reading through the New Testament (which I have read many times) when I came across a verse in John chapter 17 that jumped off the pages at me.

It wasn't the first time I had read this, but never before had I seen it this way. John 17 is an important prayer that Jesus is praying to the Father before the betrayal by Judas. In this prayer to the Father, I was

astonished to hear Jesus say in verse 4 that *He had finished* His work. I was very familiar with the words "It is finished" that Jesus spoke while hanging on the cross. Now my curiosity is piqued as I continue reading the chapter, excited to discover what Jesus was referencing.

To my amazement, Jesus's finished work was the work of discipleship! He had spent three and a half years with twelve men, training them for the most extraordinary assignment known to man. This John 17:4 revelation has changed my viewpoint on discipleship and created a hunger to delve into this topic and learn more about making disciples. If discipleship was that important to Jesus, shouldn't it be a high priority in my life? Not long after my eyes were open to this revelation, I began studying the topic throughout the Bible and buying books from respected authors on this subject.

During my studies, an interesting point I discovered is that the word *disciple* or its related words are found between 260 and 290 times (depending on the Bible translation) in contrast to the word *Christian*, appearing only three times. Do you think God is trying to tell us something?

The mission of the Church is to make disciples. We are not called to make Christians, but to make disciples, and they are different. The modern-day Church is full of Christians but very few disciples. Disciples are people who are reproducing. Christians often get saved and never grow to spiritual maturity. Just as children are not physically capable of reproducing until their bodies develop, the same is true with believers; they are not able to reproduce until they become spiritually mature.

As a senior pastor, I feel we place great emphasis and put lots of resources toward getting lost people saved, but little emphasis on developing those newborn babies into spiritual parents or disciples. Jesus was clear on what His mission was here on earth: to make disciples and redeem humanity. After the resurrection, He clearly presented the assignment to His followers. Two thousand years later, I hear those words echoing off the mountains of Galilee: "Go make disciples!"

Reading Study

1. What has been your experience with discipleship, if any?

   _____

   _____

   _____

   _____

   _____

2. According to John 17, what type of emphasis did Jesus place on discipleship?

_____

_____

_____

_____

_____

3. Explain the John 17:4 revelation the author had. What does this verse say to you?

_____

_____

_____

_____

_____

4. What is the difference between a Christian and a disciple?

_____

_____

_____

_____

_____

5. Do you feel the Church is spiritually mature as a whole? If not, what needs to occur?

_____

_____

_____

_____

_____

Bible Study Verses: Luke 5:1–11
Memory Verse: Matthew 4:19

> And he said to them, "Follow me, and I will make you fishers of men."
> (Matthew 4:19 ESV)

Background

Before Jesus began His ministry, He chose twelve men to become His followers. These men would spend the next three and a half years seeing and hearing the most amazing things imaginable. They would witness such things as the dead being raised to life, the blind eyes opened, and all kinds of diseases healed. These men began their journey by responding to the words of Jesus, "Follow Me."

Memory Verse Questions

1. Explain what it means to follow Jesus.

   _____

   _____

   _____

2. Have you ever followed the advice of a great leader? If so, what made them great leaders?

   _____

   _____

   _____

3. Do you think the disciples knew what following Jesus would entail?

   _____

   _____

   _____

4. Have you accepted the call to follow Jesus? Explain that process.

    _____

    _____

    _____

Bible Study Questions: Luke 5:1–11

1. Describe the setting on the day Jesus taught the people by the lake.

    _____

    _____

    _____

    _____

    _____

2. Do you think Jesus just randomly stepped into Simon's boat?

    _____

    _____

    _____

    _____

    _____

3. What do you think Simon thought when Jesus said to launch out into the deep?

    _____

    _____

    _____

    _____

    _____

4. Why do you think Jesus chose these fishermen to be His first disciples?

_____

_____

_____

_____

_____

5. Luke 5:11 tells us they left everything and followed Jesus. Explain the magnitude of this decision.

_____

_____

_____

_____

_____

Words from the Author

There are many reasons that people decide to become Christians. Some, like myself, were raised with a Christian influence and knew it was the right thing to do. In comparison, some people find themselves in a desperate place and decide to try Jesus. I've discovered that many of those who give Christianity a try lose faith when difficulties arise. Notice when Jesus called His disciples, He didn't ask for a trial period but a lifetime commitment. Commitments are an issue in the world we live in today. Statistics show that many marriages fail due to a lack of commitment. The wedding takes place, the vows are spoken, and two individuals begin their marriage. Unfortunately, decisions are often made to end the marriage when difficulties come. Just like a marriage, when deciding to follow Jesus, it should be an all-in approach.

"You find that the things you let go of while following Jesus were the things that were going to destroy you in the end."

—Francis Chan—

9

First and foremost, we must understand that He chose us. "You did not choose Me, but I chose you" (John 15:16 NKJV). He made the proposal, and we either accepted or rejected the offer. Becoming a follower of Christ is not a tiny assignment but will be the most significant decision anyone will ever make. Notice in the Bible study how the disciples left everything and followed Jesus. Becoming a follower of Jesus today is often nothing more than a one-time decision and continuing life as usual. It seems that oftentimes in today's society, people want to follow Jesus, but not wholeheartedly; they want to bring their own plan along with them. Imagine if Simon responded to Jesus' call to follow Him with, "I will follow if You can work it around my fishing schedule." or "I will follow if it's convenient and doesn't affect me hanging out with my buddies." Commitment to follow Jesus entails more than just attending one church service a week, but would require a complete lifestyle change. This commitment would allow these men to be with Jesus every day and would have a tremendous impact on their lives.

Discipleship is more about following Jesus than about a decision to believe. In our modern Christian era, we often emphasize deciding to believe more than committing to follow, and there is a vast difference. The Bible teaches that even the demons believe and tremble, but that doesn't make them followers of Christ. Many people decide to believe by filling out a card, raising their hand, or coming forward during a church service, but this alone doesn't constitute a commitment to follow. I'm not saying believing is not essential; I'm saying that the two are linked together. We believe and then we follow. Notice Jesus commanded us to make disciples (followers), not just believers.

Reading Study

1. Were you raised with a Christian influence? What impact did that have or not have on you becoming a follower of Christ?

   _____

   _____

   _____

   _____

2. Have you experienced a time of drifting away from God? If so, share the event. If you've never drifted away, share what you think has helped you most.

   _____

   _____

   _____

   _____

3. In your own words, give your definition of *commitment*.

_____

_____

_____

_____

_____

4. What was your initial response to being chosen to follow Christ?

_____

_____

_____

_____

_____

5. What was most difficult to walk away from when the Holy Spirit called you?

_____

_____

_____

_____

_____

6. Have you ever found yourself trying to make a deal with God when it comes to following Him?

_____

_____

_____

_____

_____

11

7. Explain the commitment you have made to personal growth and discipleship.

_____

_____

_____

_____

_____

CHAPTER 3: THE LAW OF MULTIPLICATION

Bible Study Verses: Genesis 1:11, Matthew 28:19, John 15:5–8
Memory Verse: Genesis 1:28

> And God blessed them. And God said to them, "Be fruitful and multiply and fill the earth and subdue it and have dominion over the fish of the sea and over the birds of the heavens and over every living thing that moves on the earth." (Genesis 1:28 ESV)

Background

From the beginning of creation, God's plan has always been to multiply and expand His kingdom throughout the earth. He gave Adam and Eve the command to be fruitful and multiply and to fill the earth. This command not only refers to natural reproduction, but God's desire is that we should also multiply in the spiritual. Discipleship produces multiplication, which, in essence, allows us to fulfill His command.

Memory Verse Questions

1. Do you see God's blessings in your life? Share some of the greatest blessings you've experienced.

   _____

   _____

   _____

2. How would you describe "being fruitful"?

   _____

   _____

   _____

3. Explain how God has used multiplication to spread His Word.

   _____

   _____

   _____

4. How can you see yourself applying the Law of Multiplication?

_____

_____

_____

"Working together precedes winning together...collaboration is multiplication."

—John C. Maxwell—

Bible Study Questions: Genesis 1:11, John 15:1–8, Matthew 28:19

1. Explain the similarities of the reproduction process (Genesis 1:11) regarding plants and discipleship.

_____

_____

_____

_____

_____

2. What are some of the essentials for plants and trees to reproduce?

_____

_____

_____

_____

_____

3. According to the illustration in John 15, who is Jesus referring to as the gardener, the vine, and the branch?

_____

_____

_____

_____

_____

4. Where can you see discipleship implied in John 15:1–8?

_____

_____

_____

_____

_____

Words from the Author

Adding and subtracting was hard enough to learn in first and second grade. Now third grade comes, and the teachers are handing out these cards with numbers everywhere. They called them times tables and explained the basic fundamentals of multiplication. I remember how intimidating that chart was when I first saw it, but fortunately, I had a great third-grade teacher, Mrs. Patty, who made a game out of learning it.

The Law of Multiplication has been around since the beginning of creation. On day 3 of creation, God instituted the Law of Multiplication when He said, "Let the land produce vegetation: seed-bearing plants and trees on the land that bear fruit with seed in it, according to their various kinds" (Genesis 1:11). Multiplication is seen here through the reproductive process of plants and trees bearing fruit. Notice that God implied that the fruit would have seeds, and the seed would be where multiplication begins. You may have heard the saying "You can count the seeds in an apple, but only God knows the apples in a seed." Discipleship creates multiplication by virtue of teaching and training someone who will teach and train someone else.

Notice in the Great Commission spoken by Jesus in Matthew 28:19; the KJV uses the phrase "*teach* all nations." The word *teach* in the original Greek was *matheteuo*, which has two definitions: (1) to be a disciple of one and (2) to make a disciple. Other Bible versions such as NIV translate the words "make disciples" in Matthew 28:19, which better describes the original word

matheteuo. Another interesting point concerning this word is that it represents a mathematical term. So when Jesus was standing on the mountain in Galilee, giving His disciples some final words, He used a mathematical term instructing them to multiply through discipleship. Interestingly enough, He didn't say "Go make Christians," because He knew the day would come when most people would call themselves Christians without producing fruit. Remember, seed comes from the fruit.

After Pentecost, the Church was birthed and began growing immediately. The disciples not only embraced the model Jesus had taught them, but were finding themselves leaving Jerusalem and teaching discipleship throughout the region and eventually into all the world. This message and model were spreading like wildfire. Even the most brutal persecution could not stop this move. Many were being martyred in the most gruesome ways imaginable. Rome was ruthless, burning believers alive, throwing them into the arena with wild animals, with people watching them being torn to pieces, but nothing could stop this movement.

Discipleship was taking over the world. It was estimated by the Romans that there were approximately six million followers of Christ in AD 300. It had grown at such a rate it was like multiplication! A new Roman emperor named Constantine came to power who favored the believers and stopped the persecution. Constantine stopped the brutal torture and announced to Rome that Christianity would become their national religion. Churches started being built, and organizations forming seemed like a great thing. Persecution couldn't stop the growth of the Church, but religion could. At this point, I'm convinced that the discipleship model shifted from how Jesus instituted it to how religion thought it would work best, and discipleship flatlined. Don't get me wrong, there have been pockets of true discipleship working in different parts of the world, but the model is broken as a whole.

The good news is the very last words of the Old Testament God spoke through the prophet Malachi 4:5–6 (ESV): "Behold, I will send you Elijah the prophet before the great and awesome day of the LORD comes. And he will *turn the hearts of fathers to their children and the hearts of children to their fathers*, lest I come and strike the land with a decree of utter destruction." What this is saying is discipleship will be restored in the last days! Elijah was a great disciple maker mentoring Elisha, who received the double portion anointing by doing twice as many miracles as his mentor. This is multiplica-

the POWER OF MULTIPLICATION

DAY 1: $0.01	DAY 16: $327.68
DAY 2: $0.02	DAY 17: $655.36
DAY 3: $.04	DAY 18: $1,310.72
DAY 4: $0.08	DAY 19: $2,621.44
DAY 5: $0.16	DAY 20: $5,242.88
DAY 6: $0.32	DAY 21: $10,485.76
DAY 7: $0.64	DAY 22: $20,971.52
DAY 8: $1.28	DAY 23: $41,943.04
DAY 9: $2.56	DAY 24: $83,886.08
DAY 10: $5.12	DAY 25: $167,772.16
DAY 11: $10.24	DAY 26: $335,544.32
DAY 12: $20.48	DAY 27: $671,088.64
DAY 13: $40.96	DAY 28: $1,342,177.28
DAY 14: $81.92	DAY 29: $2,684,354.56
DAY 15: $163.84	DAY 30: $5,368,709.12

tion at its best. Maybe you have heard of the phenomenon of taking a penny a day and doubling it for thirty days. (See graphic on previous page.)

Notice how slow this concept begins but has a tremendous impact with some time. Over five million dollars! Convert these numbers to people, and it's 536,870,912 people! At our church, we have witnessed this model to be accurate. If you look at day nine on the scale, it shows 252 people should have gone through disciple-ship using the one-person-a-year model. At Revolution Church in year nine, we have 283 individuals who have been through this program, which indicates that if we stay on task, we have the opportunity to see millions of people impacted through discipleship during our lifetime! Imagine how many people you can impact by committing to this process. It doesn't require the masses to bring about massive change, and it only takes one person dedicated to Jesus using the discipleship model.

2022 – 115 Disciples commissioned at Revolution church

2023 – 283 Disciples commissioned at Revolution Church

Reading Study Question

1. When did the Law of Multiplication begin? Explain.

    _____

    _____

    _____

    _____

    _____

2. How does discipleship relate to multiplication?

    _____

    _____

    _____

    _____

    _____

3. Define the Greek word *matheteuo* found in Matthew 28:19.

    _____

    _____

    _____

    _____

    _____

4. Describe how making Christianity the national religion of Rome in AD 300 impacted discipleship.

    _____

    _____

    _____

    _____

    _____

5. What do you think the prophecy in Malachi 4:5 is referring to?

_____

_____

_____

_____

_____

6. What kind of commitment will you make toward discipleship?

_____

_____

_____

_____

_____

OUR FOUNDATION

CHAPTER 4: PRAY FIRST

Bible Study Verses: Mark 1:35, Matthew 6:9–13, 1 Chronicles 4:10
Memory Verse: Psalm 5:3

> You hear my voice in the morning; at sunrise I offer my prayer and wait
> for your answer. (Psalm 5:3 GNT)

Background

Prayer is one of the most significant resources that we have as believers. Jesus, the most excellent example to follow, cherished His time alone with the Father. We will discover in this chapter the transforming power of personal devotion to the Lord and how to create essential life-changing habits related to prayer, quiet time, and Bible study.

Memory Verse Questions

1. What significance is there to praying in the morning compared to praying in the evening?

   _____

   _____

   _____

2. Describe some challenges you face when praying in the morning.

   _____

   _____

   _____

3. Prayer is essentially communicating with God. Explain in your own words why listening is just as essential as talking.

   _____

   _____

   _____

4. Do you find it difficult or easy to hear God's voice when He speaks? What can you do to make it easier?

_____

_____

_____

Bible Study Questions: Mark 1:35, Matthew 6:9–13, 1 Chronicles 4:10

1. Why do you think Jesus went to a solitary place to pray? Do you have a specific area where you pray each day?

_____

_____

_____

_____

_____

2. Notice Jesus had a busy schedule yet placed a high priority on prayer. How vital should prayer be in a disciple's life?

_____

_____

_____

_____

_____

3. In Matthew 6, when the disciples ask for instructions on how to pray, what was the first thing He said?

_____

_____

_____

_____

_____

4. What are some essential things you have learned from the Lord's Prayer?

5. Explain how you personalize the Lord's Prayer.

6. How can you apply the Prayer of Jabez to your personal life?

Words from the Author

How do you generally respond to negative situations in your life? Human nature tends to gravitate toward negativity and complaining instead of turning the condition around by being optimistic. The best way for me to live a positive life is by starting my day with prayer. As a result of incorporating specific prayers in my daily prayer time, positive situational outcomes have been obvious. There are many practical ways you can apply essential prayers of the Bible to your personal devotion. The following pages are two examples of prayers that I pray at the beginning of each day. (The Lord's Prayer and the Prayer of Jabez)

The Lord's Prayer

Relational Connection

> Our Father in Heaven,
> Hallowed be Your name.
> (Matthew 6:9)

- *Everything starts here, connecting with God relationally through prayer.*

Kingdom Connection

> Your kingdom come.
> Your will be done
> On Earth as *it is* in Heaven.
> (Matthew 6:10)

- *Pray that His kingdom is established in your heart, family, Church, and world.*
- *Pray His will be done.*

Physical Connection

> Give us this day our daily bread.
> (Matthew 6:11)

- *Pray for your daily provision.*

Spiritual Connection

> And forgive us our sins, as we have forgiven those who sin against us.
> (Matthew 6:12 NLT)

- *Pray the prayer of repentance and forgive those who have sinned against you.*

Warfare Connection

> And do not lead us into temptation,
> But deliver us from the evil one.
> (Matthew 6:13)

- *Pray God detours you from temptation.*
- *Pray every evil plan designed for you be destroyed.*

> For Yours is *the kingdom* and *the power* and *the glory* forever. Amen. (Matthew 6:9–13)

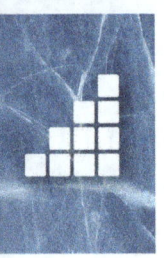

The Prayer of Jabez
1 Chronicles 4:10 (NKJV)

1. *Enlarge My Territory*

   And Jabez called on the God of Israel, saying, "Oh, that You would bless me indeed, and *enlarge my territory.*" (1 Chronicles 4:10 NKJV)

   • *Your territory is things you manage or own, such as your finances, businesses, health, ministry, retirement fund, etc.*

2. *Your Hand Be with Me*

   And Jabez called on the God of Israel, saying, "Oh, that You would bless me indeed, and enlarge my territory, that *Your hand would be with me.*"

   • *The second request is the desire for guidance and direction.*

3. *Keep Me from Evil*

   And Jabez called on the God of Israel, saying, "Oh, that You would bless me indeed, and enlarge my territory, that Your hand would be with me, and that You would keep me from evil."

   • *The third request is asking for His protection.*

4. *Keep My Past behind Me*

   And Jabez called on the God of Israel, saying, "Oh, that You would bless me indeed, and enlarge my territory, that Your hand would be with me, and that You would keep me from evil, *that I may not cause pain!*"

   • *Jabez's name means "sorrow" or "one who causes pain." The final request is to pray that we never revert to whom we used to be.*

   So *God granted him what he requested.* (1 Chronicles 4:10 NKJV)

There have been lots of studies related to human habits. Some studies have shown that it only takes twenty-one days to develop a habit, while others have indicated it takes much longer. Regardless if it takes twenty-one days or one hundred days—to form a habit, that is beside the point I'm trying to make. The fact is that every habit begins at the same place, and that's on day one. We can talk about prayer and think about prayer, but we must ultimately start this process of communicating with God. Developing the daily prayer habit is essential in every believer's life.

Reading Study Question

1. Explain how you normally respond to a crisis.

    _____

    _____

    _____

    _____

    _____

2. Does the way you respond impact those around you? Explain.

    _____

    _____

    _____

    _____

    _____

3. On a scale of 1–10, how would you rate your prayer life?

    _____

    _____

    _____

    _____

    _____

4. What are your greatest obstacles when it comes to prayer?

    _____

    _____

    _____

    _____

    _____

5. Jesus didn't want our prayer life to be robotic, yet He did give examples of how to pray. How can you use these prayers without them seeming ritualistic?

_____

_____

_____

_____

_____

6. Explain what you can do to improve your personal prayer life.

_____

_____

_____

_____

_____

"To be a Christian without prayer is no more possible than to be alive without breathing."

—Martin Luther King Jr.—

CHAPTER 5: BIBLICAL APPLICATION

Bible Study Verses: Joshua 1:8, 2 Timothy 3 14–17, Proverbs 3:1–2
Memory Verse:

> Be diligent to present yourself approved to God, a worker who does not
> need to be ashamed, rightly dividing the word of truth. (2 Timothy 2:15
> NKJV)

Background

This chapter will provide several methods and approaches that will be helpful in Bible study and general application. Also included in the chapter will be an in-depth look at the subject "Interpreting the Bible."

Memory Verse Questions

1. What do you think of when you hear the word *diligent*?

   _____

   _____

   _____

2. Would you consider yourself diligent when it comes to the things of God?

   _____

   _____

   _____

3. What does it mean to divide the Word of God rightly?

   _____

   _____

   _____

4. Why is it important to know the Word of God?

_____

_____

_____

5. What are your current methods of studying the scriptures?

_____

_____

_____

Bible Study Questions: Joshua 1:8, 2 Timothy 3:14–17, Proverbs 3:1–2

1. In Joshua's inaugural speech, why do you think he was so adamant about knowing and observing the Law?

_____

_____

_____

_____

_____

2. According to Joshua 1:8, prosperity and success were conditional on what?

_____

_____

_____

_____

_____

3. Describe what it means to meditate day and night on His Word.

_____

_____

_____

_____

4. Paul, in his second letter to Timothy, chapter 3, explained the evil conditions during the last days and emphasized knowing the scriptures. Why is this?

_____

_____

_____

_____

_____

5. What did Paul describe as some of the benefits of knowing the scriptures?

_____

_____

_____

_____

_____

6. What are some of the benefits mentioned in Proverbs 3:1–2 related to not forgetting His Law?

_____

_____

_____

_____

_____

Words from the Author

The Bible contains various authors and writing styles, such as history, letters, prophetic writings, poetry, wise sayings, apocalyptic lettering, and much more. These biblical writers were moved upon by the Holy Spirit and inspired to pen what God wanted to say. The Bible consists of sixty-six books and forty authors, written over 1,500 years on three continents. It's nothing shy of a miracle that God preserved His Word and has made it available to virtually everyone in the world. When I was young, the King James Version was primarily the only version I was taught from. Today there are many good Bible translations to choose from, but I wouldn't recommend studying from paraphrased versions since they are not actual Bible translations.

The common thing you will find with every mature Christian is that they will have a regular Bible reading plan. Believers need to study the Bible actively. The Bible teaches us everything we need to know about God and life. A Christian not knowing the Bible would be like a chef not knowing a recipe or a pilot not knowing the FAA requirements, which could be detrimental to your health. Remember Satan's deceptive tactic against Jesus in the wilderness was twisting God's Word. He's a master manipulator and deceiver, but Jesus was more than he bargained for. Jesus responded to Satan's deception with three words, "It is written," followed by the exact Word of God. Knowing the Word and living by it will be extremely helpful in your discipleship journey. It will also be beneficial for life in general. As you consume God's Word and become a student of it, you'll find that everything you do will be filtered through your biblical conscience. Have you noticed the check you get in your spirit when something is done or said that contradicts God's Word? Having the Word of God embedded in your mind is invaluable in your walk with Jesus and will keep you grounded in the truth. David said in Psalm 119:11, "I have hidden your Word in my heart that I may not sin against you." Obviously, knowing the Word doesn't always mean you will obey it. Before David committed adultery with Bathsheba, how many times do you think he heard the sixth commandment God gave Moses? I'm sure it rang in his mind several times because the commands were hidden in his heart. This is a reminder that knowledge without application produces a negative outcome. James said that those who know to do good and do it not, to him, it is a sin. Look at how God responds to neglecting His Law:

> My people are destroyed for lack of knowledge. Because you have rejected knowledge, I also will reject you from being priest for Me; Because you have forgotten the Law of your God, I also will forget your children. (Hosea 4:6 NKJV)

Several different Bible reading plans are available on various apps online. Most of today's phones can access these for free. You can place reading reminders that will alert you and keep track of your reading. You can do a very in-depth New Testament study in one year by reading only five chapters a week and creating a personal journal/commentary. You can use this model not only for your personal growth, but also to disciple others. In the Olivet Discourse in Matthew 24, the disciples ask Jesus for a sign of the end of time, and He says, "Watch and be not deceived." The people who know their God and His Word will not easily fall into this trap but will be able to warn others.

Reading Study Question

1. How many books are in the Bible?

   _____

   _____

   _____

   _____

   _____

2. What is your favorite book of the Bible?

   _____

   _____

   _____

   _____

   _____

3. What is the difference between a paraphrased and translated Bible?

   _____

   _____

   _____

   _____

   _____

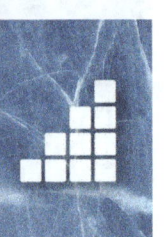

4. Why is it vital for you to know the Word of God?

_____

_____

_____

_____

_____

5. What tactic did Satan use to tempt Jesus?

_____

_____

_____

_____

_____

6. What did Hosea say God's people were destroyed for?

"In our prayers, we talk to God, in our Bible study, God talks to us, and we had better let God do most of the talking."

—Dwight L. Moody—

_____

_____

_____

_____

_____

7. Explain what Bible reading plan you are using.

_____

_____

_____

_____

_____

CHAPTER 6: EXPRESSIONS OF WORSHIP

Bible Study Verses: 1 Peter 2:5, Psalm 63:4, Psalm 95:6
Memory Verse: John 4:24 (KJV)

> God is a Spirit: and they that worship him must worship him in Spirit and in truth. (John 4:24 KJV)

Background

The desire to worship God is part of our intricate design. Being created in God's image explains humanity's desire for worship. This chapter will discuss the importance of our worship being directed toward God, not the idols of this world.

Memory Verse Questions

1. In John chapter 4, who was Jesus talking to when he made this statement?

   _____

   _____

   _____

2. Where did the Samaritans and Jews worship?

   _____

   _____

   _____

3. Why didn't they worship together?

   _____

   _____

   _____

4. What was Jesus emphasizing when He said "God is Spirit"?

_____

_____

_____

5. How did Jesus say true worshipers would worship the Father?

_____

_____

_____

Bible Study Questions: 1 Peter 2:5, Psalm 63:4, Psalm 95:6

1. Why do you think Jesus is referred to as a Living Stone?

_____

_____

_____

_____

_____

2. What does Peter refer believers to in 1 Peter 2:5?

_____

_____

_____

_____

_____

3. As we grow into a spiritual house, a holy priesthood, what are our expectations?

_____

_____

_____

_____

_____

4. Explain spiritual sacrifices that would be acceptable to God…also sacrifices that would not be acceptable.

_____

_____

_____

_____

_____

5. Name the different bodily postures expressed during worship in Psalm 63:4 and Psalm 95:6.

_____

_____

_____

_____

_____

6. Psalm 63:4 indicates private worship, whereas Psalm 95:6 suggests corporate worship. Why do we need both?

_____

_____

_____

_____

_____

7. Do you find it easy or challenging to worship by raising your hands or bowing? Explain.

_____

_____

_____

_____

_____

Words from the Author

Being raised in the Bible Belt, attending weekend worship services seemed like the normal thing to do as a young boy. You could expect several things: Sunday school, a greeting from the pastor, three or four songs, an offering, prayer, a sermon, and an altar call. I was under the assumption the worship part of service was during the singing since that's when some would lift their hands in praise. As I began studying the Word and maturing, I discovered that the entire service was worship. I realized that you don't have to be in a church building to worship God. Worship is simply an expression of thanksgiving and adoration for God.

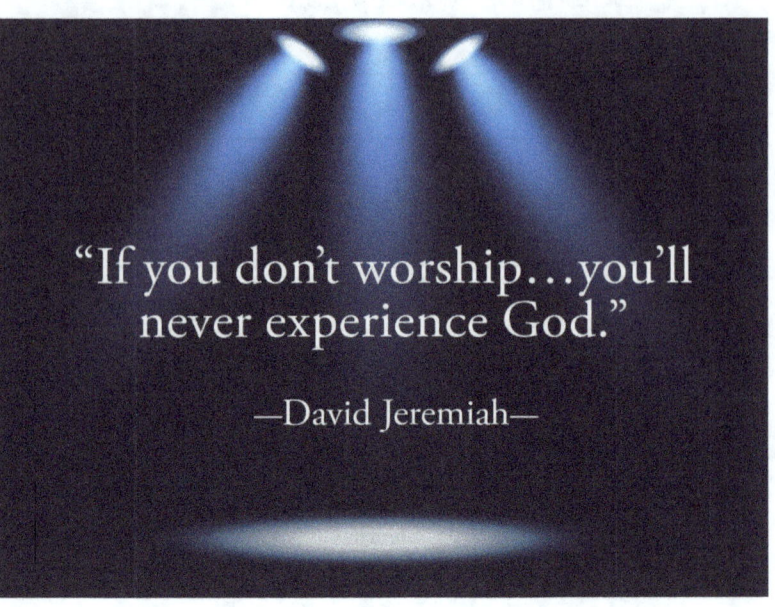

"If you don't worship…you'll never experience God."

—David Jeremiah—

When the Samaritan woman asked Jesus about worship, He said true worship isn't about being in a specific geographic location but about worshiping in spirit and in truth. This type of acceptable worship can only come from a transformed heart. Ezekiel prophesied about the transformed heart. "I will give you a new heart and put a new spirit in you; I will remove from you your heart of stone and give you a heart of flesh" (Ezekiel 36:26 NIV). Prior to accepting Jesus, we had the Adamic nature that wouldn't allow us to worship in spirit and truth. Only after our conversion could we worship God correctly.

Two types of worship are essential for all believers.

Individual Worship. This is your one-on-one time with God. I like to spend this time early in the morning. For me, it usually consists of prayer and devotion time. There's no better way to start your day than getting in His presence and acknowledging Him in your life. As I worship and recognize Him as protector and provider, He shows up in spirit and truth. This is an incredible experience that God wants all of His children to enjoy. During these times of individual worship, I've had the Spirit give me direction for the day or sometimes bring something to my memory that I had forgotten. I consider this time of worship my spiritual gym time. This strengthens my spirit and my walk with Jesus. Just like the natural gym, consistency builds muscle, not the sporadic visits. The second type of worship that is essential is corporate worship.

Corporate Worship. We gather for corporate worship on Sundays, the first day of the week. Just as individual worship is vital, corporate worship is equally important. This is our time to come together with the Body of Christ and corporately celebrate Jesus; what an exciting time to pray, sing, and open the Word as one. It's in these settings where God said He would command the blessings

of heaven on believers. Believers who miss these worship gatherings are being robbed of God's gift in their life. The author of Hebrews places a strong emphasis on gathering together. "And let us not neglect our meeting together, as some people do, but encourage one another, especially now that the day of his return is drawing near" (Hebrews 10:25 NLT).

In April 2020, a nationwide mandate across the United States did not allow churches to gather because of the COVID-19 pandemic. We were fortunate to have been live streaming our services before this mandate occurred. Our Church, like most, asked the congregation to watch from home until the stay-at-home order was lifted. It was good to have the online service, but it wasn't the same as gathering together. When the order was raised, I was saddened to see how many brothers and sisters didn't return to Church. Many of the members said they would continue watching from home for a while, but unfortunately, over two years later, several are still not back. This saddens me because I realize what they are missing out on is essential to their spiritual well-being. We absolutely, without question, need each other! There's something supernatural about being in the same room with fellow believers worshiping God as one.

Numerous times I've shown up to church heavily burdened about a situation, and before the first worship song was completed, the weight was lifted, and I was recharged. Everyone worships differently, and churches have different styles or different flavors. I've discovered that it's not the style of song that determines my worship, but the attitude of my heart. I personally prefer upbeat contemporary music, but I can worship with a slow hymn just as well. When I worship, I'm generally very expressive, such as lifting my hands in praise and occasionally dancing if appropriate. I've heard some people say that's emotionalism, but I'm pretty sure God's okay with me being excited when I worship. How would some of those people respond to King David's style of worship? Being around sports and ball fields most of my life, I've seen many people express excitement when their team does something special. Imagine what our worship services would look like if we expressed excitement because of what Jesus has done for us. Don't get me wrong, I'm not advocating for a particular style of worship; I'm just encouraging everyone to worship in spirit and truth.

Reading Study Question

1. Describe your church experience growing up.

    _____

    _____

    _____

    _____

    _____

2. What do you think of when you hear the word *worship*?

    _____

    _____

    _____

    _____

    _____

3. How did Jesus say we were to worship God?

    _____

    _____

    _____

    _____

    _____

4. Before we can worship God acceptably, what must happen?

    _____

    _____

    _____

    _____

    _____

5. What are some different ways you can worship God individually?

_____

_____

_____

_____

_____

6. Why is it vital to gather with the Body of Christ to worship?

_____

_____

_____

_____

_____

7. Explain how corporate worship has been a blessing to you.

_____

_____

_____

_____

_____

CHAPTER 7: FAST-FORWARD

Bible Study Verses: Matthew 6:16–18, Mark 9:17–29, Luke 4:1–13 (NKJV)
Memory Verse:

> So after they had fasted and prayed, they placed their hands on them and sent them off. (Acts 13:3 NIV)

Background

Fasting has been an essential discipline practiced by God's people from the earliest writings of the Old Testament. In this chapter, we will discover biblical ways to fast and pray and what you can expect from applying these principles.

Memory Verse Questions

1. What are the two spiritual disciplines mentioned in the memory verse?

   _____

   _____

   _____

2. Who were the two men sent on the mission?

   _____

   _____

   _____

3. Who called the men to go on this assignment?

   _____

   _____

   _____

4. What preceded the calling?

_____

_____

_____

5. Other than prayer and fasting, what was the third action taken before sending Barnabas and Saul on the mission?

_____

_____

_____

Bible Study Questions: Matthew 6:16–18, Mark 9:17–29, Luke 4:1–13 (NKJV)

1. While you are on a personal fast, what are some of the things Jesus said to do in Matthew 6:16–18?

_____

_____

_____

_____

_____

2. Why did the man bring his son to Jesus in Mark 9:17–18?

_____

_____

_____

_____

_____

3. How did Jesus respond to His disciples?

_____

_____

_____

_____

_____

4. Explain what happened when Jesus addressed the man's son.

_____

_____

_____

_____

_____

5. How did Jesus answer the disciples when they asked why they couldn't cast out the demon?

_____

_____

_____

_____

_____

6. Why do you think it's significant that Jesus fasted before beginning His ministry?

_____

_____

_____

_____

_____

7. Do you think fasting gives you an edge when praying about something? Why or why not?

_____

_____

_____

_____

_____

Words from the Author

Fasting is a foundational discipline that we often seem to skim over or totally ignore. I would venture to say that any topic mentioned in the Bible over seventy times deserves plenty of airtime. I'll be the first to say that fasting isn't something I look forward to because it requires me to say no to something I love: eating! Our Church always participates in a twenty-one-day fast at the beginning of each year, which I'm convinced has contributed to years of continued growth. Following one of our corporate fasts, ninety people were miraculously saved the following month.

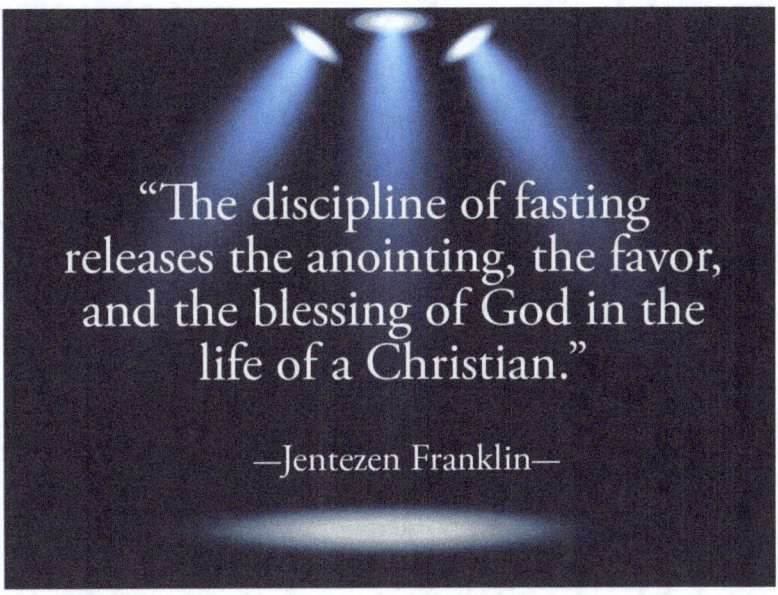

"The discipline of fasting releases the anointing, the favor, and the blessing of God in the life of a Christian."

—Jentezen Franklin—

In our Bible study for this chapter, we see a desperate man bring his son to Jesus, asking Him to cure the son. This man explains that he had brought his son to the disciples, but they couldn't help him. Jesus, apparently upset, says, "O faithless and perverse generation, how long will I be with you and put up with you?" Jesus asked for the son and rebuked the demon tormenting him, and the son was immediately cured. Privately, the disciples came to Jesus and asked why they couldn't heal him, and He responded that this kind does not leave except through prayer and fasting. Understand that certain things we pray for that seem to be going nowhere may need fasting added.

There are many types of fasts throughout Scripture, including total fast, partial fast, corporate fast, and the twenty-one-day fast that Daniel completed. Fasting should always be taken very seriously and covered in prayer beforehand. It's essential to speak with your doctor before fasting, especially extended fasts, to make sure there are no

health concerns to be aware of. Occasional fasting can also have health benefits by allowing your body to detox from all the foods with additives and preservatives we frequently eat. The first few days can be the hardest during an extended fast. Being a coffee drinker, I get headaches and have hunger pains for about two days. Afterward, I feel better as my body adjusts to the fast. I've noticed during the extended fast that my sense of smell and hearing dramatically improves.

Prayer-led fasting obviously isn't harmful to you, or God wouldn't have told us to do it. Three people are mentioned in the Bible that fasted for forty straight days: Moses, Elijah, and Jesus. Notice before Jesus began His ministry, He spent forty days and nights in the wilderness fasting, praying, and being tempted by Satan. Matthew 4:1 tells us that after the fast, He was hungry, but not until it was over. When Jesus came out of the wilderness, He was ready for ministry and prepared for a breakthrough! Is there any area of your life where you need a breakthrough? Pray about a fast and see if the Lord leads you in that direction. I believe you'll see extraordinary results just as I have. Make fasting part of your devotional life, even if it's an occasional meal that you set aside. If you're not currently involved in a corporate fast, join us at riorevolutionchurch.com next year in January for a twenty-one-day fast. There are lots of resources on the different types of fasts that you can research. I'm praying that as you begin fasting, there will be special prayers answered and incredible doors opened. It'll be like you are moving fast-forward!

Reading Study Question

1. Is fasting something you hear spoken of often? Explain why or why not.

    _____

    _____

    _____

    _____

    _____

2. How often do you fast, if ever?

    _____

    _____

    _____

    _____

    _____

3. What does fasting require you to say no to?

_____

_____

_____

_____

_____

4. Why couldn't the disciples heal the man's son?

_____

_____

_____

_____

_____

5. How did Jesus answer the disciples when they came privately asking why they couldn't heal the boy?

_____

_____

_____

_____

_____

6. What are some of the different types of fasts throughout the Bible?

_____

_____

_____

_____

_____

7. Name the people in the Bible who fasted for forty days.

_____

_____

_____

_____

_____

8. Write down an area in your life where you'd like to see a breakthrough and begin to pray and fast for it.

_____

_____

_____

_____

_____

OUR PERSONALITY

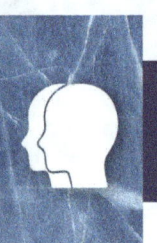

CHAPTER 8: DESIGNED WITH PURPOSE

Bible Study Verses: Genesis 1:26–31, John 15:16, Ephesians 1:11
Memory Verse:

> For we are his workmanship, created in Christ Jesus for good works, which God prepared beforehand, that we should walk in them. (Ephesians 2:10 ESV)

Background

Purpose and identity are two subjects that have generated lots of questions throughout time. This chapter will explore what Scripture says about our unique design and the importance of discovering our purpose.

Memory Verse Questions

1. What role does an architect play in a building project?

   _____

   _____

   _____

2. Of all the different characteristics of the human race, what is one that all have in common?

   _____

   _____

   _____

3. Of all the billions of people on earth, no two people are exactly alike. Why do you think God created everyone differently?

   _____

   _____

   _____

4. Do you feel that God has gifted you in some areas where you can help others?

_____

_____

_____

5. Write down at least two verses that support a predestined plan for your life. What do you feel is the key to fulfilling this plan?

_____

_____

_____

6. Explain how accepting Christ was part of God's predetermined plan for your life. What are the most notable changes in you since being born again?

"Every time you look in the mirror remember that God created you and that everything He creates is beautiful and good!"

—Joyce Meyer—

_____

_____

_____

Bible Study Questions: Genesis 1:26–31, John 15:16, Ephesians 1:11

1. What does it mean to be created in God's image?

_____

_____

_____

_____

_____

2. According to Genesis 1:26–31, what are some of the responsibilities God gave the human race?

_____

_____

_____

_____

_____

3. What correlation is there between Genesis 1:28 and Matthew 28:19? What role are you to play in these commands?

_____

_____

_____

_____

_____

4. Describe the feelings of being appointed to a task by God.

_____

_____

_____

_____

_____

5. John 15:16 makes it clear that you have a unique purpose. In your own words, describe what it means to bear fruit.

_____

_____

_____

_____

_____

6. What relation does bearing fruit have with answered prayers?

_____

_____

_____

_____

_____

7. Ephesians 1:11 not only speaks of being chosen but also being predestined. Explain in your own words what that means to you.

_____

_____

_____

_____

_____

8. Have you ever had the privilege of choosing someone for an important task? What went into your selection process? Did they meet your expectations?

_____

_____

_____

_____

_____

Words from the Author

Many times, the image we have of ourselves has been tainted by several snapshots from our past. People generally struggle with seeing themselves doing anything more remarkable than they currently do. You are probably sitting down as you read this book, wondering, *Am I fulfilling my God-given purpose?* Someone once said that three people are sitting in your chair: the person you see, the person others see, and the person God sees. God sees you as someone with a special purpose that only you can fulfill. Imagine, of the 7.4 billion people in the world, no two individuals are exactly the same. Many go through life searching for their purpose and place, only to find themselves frustrated with another dead-end road. The most excellent satisfaction in

life is knowing your God-given assignment. Your mission in life can only be found in the living Word of God. "And God blessed them. And God said to them, '*Be fruitful and multiply* and *fill the earth and subdue* it and *have dominion* over the fish of the sea and over the birds of the heavens and over every living thing that moves on the earth'" (Genesis 1:28 ESV). This verse spoke not only to Adam and Eve, but to all humanity. Notice that this assignment presents three fundamental keys related to our purpose in life. The first key mentioned is to be fruitful and multiply. The second key is to fill and subdue the earth. The third is to have dominion over things on this earth. We can better understand these items by allowing the Bible to interpret itself.

Fruitful and multiply. Being fruitful can be interpreted in many different ways and rightfully so. One definition of *fruitful* is producing a good result—very productive. In every area of our lives, there should be an emphasis placed on producing good results. Have you noticed that Christians often work hard on producing good results in their spiritual life, but don't seem to give equal effort in everyday living? Imagine the impact we would have on society if we produced good results with everything we touched. How important is it to be fruitful in daily activities, such as building relationships, parenting, work, health, exercise, eating habits, managing finances, and household tasks, to name a few? A great example of a family who applied this principle was Abraham and Sarah. Genesis 13:2 tells us that they had become highly fruitful and experienced multiplication with their livestock, gold, and silver. To be fruitful requires work and effort. Not many people

see this kind of result without being intentional and disciplined. God's first assignment for Adam signifies the importance of being fruitful!

Fill and subdue. The Hebrew word used in Genesis 1:28 for *fill* is *male*, meaning to fill or replenish. Notice how Adam and Eve applied these commands in their everyday life while living in the Garden of Eden. *Subdue* means "to control or bring into subjection," which is exactly what we do when working in a garden. In my childhood years, I would help my grandmother in the garden. One of the most enjoyable experiences in gardening is planting seeds. We would work tirelessly preparing the soil for planting, and finally, it was a huge relief to lay out the rows and plant the seeds.

Unfortunately, the work wasn't over, but was only beginning. In just a few weeks, you would see the plants burst through the ground in perfect rows. Unfortunately, along with the plants came the dreaded weeds, which required constant attention. We used a garden tiller to uproot the weeds between the rows of plants, but you had to be careful not to get too close because you risked uprooting the plant. That's where the labor-intensive hoe was required to remove the weeds growing close to the plants. I was taught an early lesson about how to subdue the weeds in my grandmother's garden. This same lesson applies to our everyday life regarding keeping the weeds out.

Dominion. The Hebrew word used in Genesis 1:28 for *dominion* is *radah*: to rule, dominate. Interestingly enough, God placed Adam and Eve in a position to rule not only over the fish, birds, and animals, but over their fleshly desires. The opposite of having dominion is living in slavery. God designed

us as sons and daughters to rule and reign here on this earth, not to live a life of slavery. Adam and Eve had been given dominion over the serpent, but he realized if he could convince them to eat the forbidden fruit, their dominion would be relinquished, and he would take possession. This act of disobedience carried tremendous consequences of not only losing authority in the garden, but also causing separation from God. The great news is that Jesus came and reclaimed our lost dominion. In Matthew 28:18, Jesus left this statement with the disciples: "All power in Heaven and earth has been given to me." This dominion that Jesus took back is available to all of us who believe.

Reading Study

1. Do you feel like God has designed you for something different from what you currently do?

    _____

    _____

    _____

    _____

    _____

2. How is God using your past to help others?

    _____

    _____

    _____

    _____

    _____

3. Where can we find our assignment for life?

    _____

    _____

    _____

    _____

    _____

4. Name the three assignments God gave all humanity in Genesis 1:28.

_____

_____

_____

_____

_____

5. Name some different ways of being fruitful.

_____

_____

_____

_____

_____

6. What areas in your life could you be more fruitful? What action can you take that will provide meaningful results?

_____

_____

_____

_____

_____

7. Why did Jesus make the statement, "All power in heaven and earth has been given to me"?

_____

_____

_____

_____

_____

CHAPTER 9: TRANSFORMING YOUR THOUGHTS

Bible Study Verses: Philippians 4:7–8, 2 Corinthians 10:4–5, Colossians 3:2–5
Memory Verse:

> And do not be conformed to this world, but be transformed by the renewing of your mind, that you may prove what is that good and acceptable and perfect will of God. (Romans 12:2 NKJV)

Background

The human brain is an incredibly complicated organ that has enormous untapped potential. During this chapter, we will discover how to effectively program our thoughts to set us on the right trajectory.

Memory Verse Questions

1. Describe the difference between *conformed* and *transformed*.

   _____

   _____

   _____

2. What are some subtle ways this world shapes our thoughts?

   _____

   _____

   _____

3. How can our minds be renewed?

   _____

   _____

   _____

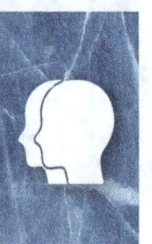

4. Give an example of how you have personally seen this renewal process work.

_____

_____

_____

Bible Study Questions: Philippians 4:7–8, 2 Corinthians 10:4–5, Colossians 3:2–5

1. In Philippians 4:7, what did Paul say would guard your minds in Christ Jesus?

_____

_____

_____

_____

_____

2. Name the things Paul instructed the Philippians to think about.

_____

_____

_____

_____

_____

3. What are some things that we shouldn't think about?

_____

_____

_____

_____

_____

4. Explain what it means to take captive your thoughts and make them obedient to Christ (2 Corinthians 10:5).

_____

_____

_____

_____

_____

5. In Colossians 3:2, Paul states, "Set your minds on things above not on earthly things." Explain in your own words the contrast between the two.

_____

_____

_____

_____

_____

6. Paul writes in verse 3 that you've metaphorically died. Explain what part of us needs to die (Reference verse 5).

_____

_____

_____

_____

_____

7. Why is it essential to put earthly nature to death every day?

_____

_____

_____

_____

_____

Words from the Author

The human mind has capabilities that reach far beyond our understanding. Experts say that the average person only uses 10 percent of their brain's potential. Studies have also shown that the human brain begins development three weeks after conception and is a lifelong process. During this early development, medical science has discovered that more than 250,000 neurons are added every minute. At birth, studies show that almost all the neurons the brain will ever have are present. Throughout life, the brain is developed by exposure to multiple circumstances and events. These events are responsible for storing information and forming neural pathways, which some refer to as brain grooves. These pathways are visible to the eye and developed due to everyday habits.

As we know, patterns can be good or bad depending on our choices. The great news is that we can change bad habits and bad thoughts. This is why Paul said in Romans that we should transform our minds or, in other words, change our habits. To change a habit, one only needs to change his thoughts. By intentionally reprogramming our thoughts, noticeable changes in our actions will soon follow. Paul instructed us in Philippians 4:8 to think about lovely, pure, true, admirable, and excellent things. Over the years, I've noticed people who aren't happy and are pessimistic by nature struggle with negative thinking. Many people talk themselves out of doing anything significant for God because of their small thinking. God wants to use you in tremen-

dous ways, but this will be impossible without transforming our thinking. When Peter was called to follow Jesus, he had no idea

> "People living in the vanity of their own mind not only destroy themselves, but far too often, they bring destruction to others around them."
>
> —Joyce Meyer—

that someday God would use him to effectively stand and speak to men and women of great intellect. The impact that Peter would have when he spoke was phenomenal. The highly intellectual crowds were astonished at the boldness of his presentations. I'm sure Peter often resisted the enemy when he placed thoughts in his mind such as "You're just a fisherman." or "You're not qualified." "You can't effectively communicate with these people of influence." We will never be exempt from having similar thoughts, but we have been given the power to either retain or delete them. These negative thoughts will eventually surface and become negative actions if we retain them. Every thought that enters our mind should be run through the filter of God's Word to determine whether we discard or keep them. When the enemy tells you why you're not qualified to lead others, remind him that you can do all things through Christ Jesus.

1. What percentage of the brain do experts say we use?

    _____

    _____

    _____

    _____

    _____

2. At what point does our brain stop developing?

    _____

    _____

    _____

    _____

    _____

3. How are neural pathways formed?

    _____

    _____

    _____

    _____

    _____

4. Do we have the ability to change these pathways? Explain.

    _____

    _____

    _____

    _____

    _____

5. Describe how our thinking relates to our actions.

_____

_____

_____

_____

_____

6. What control do you have over thoughts that enter your mind?

_____

_____

_____

_____

_____

7. Name an area in your thinking that needs to be reprogrammed.

_____

_____

_____

_____

_____

8. If there were no thoughts of failure, what would you be doing differently today?

_____

_____

_____

_____

_____

9. Explain how you can impact others by thinking about the positive and not the negative.

_____

_____

_____

_____

_____

CHAPTER 10: WHAT ABOUT ME?

Bible Study Verses: Mark 10:42–45, John 13:1–17
Memory Verse:

> Then Jesus said to his disciples, "Whoever wants to be my disciple must deny themselves and take up their cross and follow me." (Matthew 16:24 NIV)

Background

The culture of Jesus's day was all about honoring men. It was clear where you ranked in society by how you were honored among the people. Honor was shown by things such as where you sat at a banquet table or your position in the temple. Jesus changed this concept radically by becoming the greatest servant leader ever to live.

Memory Verse Questions

1. What is the prerequisite to becoming a disciple of Jesus?

   _____

   _____

   _____

2. What does it mean to deny yourself?

   _____

   _____

   _____

3. Share some examples of how society endorses self-promotion.

   _____

   _____

   _____

4. How did Jesus demonstrate self-denial?

_____

_____

_____

5. What does it mean for you to "take up your cross"?

_____

_____

_____

6. Why did Jesus make it personal and reference it as "*your* cross"?

_____

_____

_____

7. Of the three requirements for being His disciple, which is most difficult for you? Why?

_____

_____

_____

Bible Study Questions: Mark 10:42–45, John 13:1–17

1. In Mark 10:42–45, what example did Jesus give describing their current Gentile leadership?

_____

_____

_____

_____

_____

2. What culture change did He inject in verse 43?

_____

_____

_____

_____

_____

3. What path does Jesus say will lead to greatness?

_____

_____

_____

_____

_____

4. Is this a method that you see taught in modern-day society? Why or why not?

_____

_____

_____

_____

_____

5. What area in your life can you become a better servant leader?

_____

_____

_____

_____

_____

6. John 13:1–17: explain the setting.

_____

_____

_____

_____

_____

7. In verse 4, explain how Jesus lays out the perfect example of servant leadership.

_____

_____

_____

_____

_____

8. How can we take on the role of a servant in modern-day society?

> "The world says love yourself, grab all you can, follow your heart. Jesus says deny yourself, grab your cross, and follow me."
>
> —Francis Chan—

_____

_____

_____

_____

_____

Words from the Author: Matthew 20:26

In the United States, free enterprise, entrepreneurship, and climbing the ladder of success are as much American as baseball, apple pie, hot dogs, and Chevrolet. Unfortunately, climbing the ladder of success often encourages selfishness. Notice the first requirement to being one of Jesus's disciples is self-denial. I've found this to be the most challenging task in pursuing Christlikeness.

In my early forties, my wife, Connie, and I had a thriving business growing exponentially. We were making great money and were able to pay off all of our debt. We had the privilege of taking family vacations to beautiful places like Hawaii, Alaska, and Mexico. We

were living the American dream and helping fund our Church's mission projects. Little did we know that our life was on the verge of significant change. God was preparing Connie and me to surrender our selfish ambitions and answer the call to shepherd His flock.

"Wow, I'm forty-three years old with no seminary degree and no pastoral experience! Are You sure You're talking to the right guy?" Yes, was His answer, and now I'm faced with questions about our business, family, and finances. And then the big question, What about me? How will this affect me? What will I have to give up? Unlike the worldly view of climbing the ladder of success, Jesus teaches that the ladder of success is not climbing up, but descending into greatness through serving others.

An example of this can be seen in the life of Mother Teresa. She had become successful first as a schoolteacher and then by being promoted to principal of her school. Mother Teresa, at thirty-six years old, was not content with success as many may see it. She decided to leave her place of employment working for the school system and go to work for the poor and needy kids on the street. Mother Teresa began gathering slum children and teaching them under a tree.

Two years later, she opened her first school in Kolkata for slum children. Her target was helping those who were unwanted, abandoned, and unloved. She eventually set up over 570 homes for the poor in more than 125 countries. Mother Teresa has been honored with many awards, including the Nobel Prize for peace in 1979 along with India's highest Civilian Award, *Bharat Ratna*. I've discovered that the most incredible life satisfaction comes through giving and serving rather than receiving and being served. This concept is at the core of discipleship and was best illustrated by Jesus as He demonstrated servant leadership during His life on earth and even more in His death. As Jesus was nearing the end of His life on earth, we find Him spending quality time with the disciples and giving them some final teachings. The setting of the Last Supper is Jesus gathering with His disciples for their last meal together. They had probably sat together and eaten several thousand times over the previous three years, but this time was different. This would be Jesus's last opportunity to share an important message in such an intimate setting. What lesson would Jesus choose to teach? The topic could have been on a deep theological subject such as eschatology or predestination.

Interestingly enough, Jesus, after having the meal, proceeds with an illustration that would be so counterculture that even His disciples would struggle with His actions. Jesus, after the meal, rises from His seat, not to dismiss everyone, but to use this occasion to drive home an important message. He takes His robe, lays it aside, and proceeds to take a servant's towel and wraps it around His waist. He then pours water into a bowl and begins washing the disciples' feet. Jesus was leaving with His disciples the importance of serving others. An illustration such as this only reinforced all of His prior teachings of putting others ahead of ourselves. Peter had a problem with this concept and even verbalized his thoughts, saying, "You shall never wash my feet."

The response to Peter was, "Unless I wash your feet, you shall have no part with Me," which changed Peter's viewpoint. Jesus gave the perfect example of discipleship: To be great, you must first become a servant to all.

1. Have you ever found yourself in the culture rat race of chasing the American dream? If so, explain.

    _____

    _____

    _____

    _____

    _____

2. Name some areas in your life where you have struggled with selfishness.

    _____

    _____

    _____

    _____

    _____

3. List some characteristics of greatness.

    _____

    _____

    _____

    _____

    _____

4. Have you ever considered ways of serving more in your Church? In your community? In other areas? Explain.

    _____

    _____

    _____

    _____

    _____

5. What do you consider the biggest hindrance to serving?

_____

_____

_____

_____

_____

6. Give two examples of how Jesus placed serving others in high regard.

_____

_____

_____

_____

_____

7. At the Last Supper, why do you think Peter didn't want Jesus to wash his feet?

_____

_____

_____

_____

_____

8. Are you inspired by Jesus to serve others? If so, name some specific ways in which you can do so.

_____

_____

_____

_____

_____

OUR REDEMPTION

CHAPTER 11: SIN AND REDEMPTION

Bible Study Verses: Romans 3:9–24, Romans 6:12–18, Proverbs 28:13
Memory Verse:

> If you openly declare that Jesus is Lord and believe in your heart that God raised him from the dead, you will be saved. For it is with your heart that you believe and are justified, and it is with your mouth that you profess your faith and are saved. (Romans 10:9–10 NLT)

Background

Sin is simply missing the mark. Every human being has inherently received the sin nature that has been passed down since the fall of man. There is one fix for sin, and His name is Jesus Christ. This chapter focuses on the solution for sin.

Memory Verse Question

1. Explain what it means to "openly declare" something.

    _____

    _____

    _____

2. What is the difference between believing in Jesus and making Him Lord?

    _____

    _____

    _____

3. Why do you think believing in the resurrection is essential to salvation?

    _____

    _____

    _____

4. Describe the importance of professing your faith.

_____

_____

_____

5. Explain in your own words the process of being saved.

_____

_____

_____

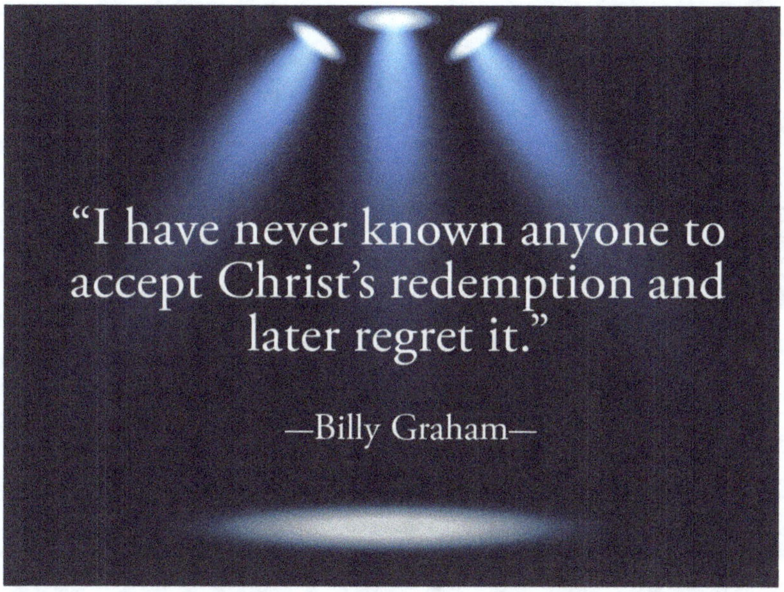

"I have never known anyone to accept Christ's redemption and later regret it."

—Billy Graham—

Bible Study Questions: Romans 3:9–24, Romans 6:12–18, Proverbs 28:13

1. What does Romans 3:9 tell us about sin?

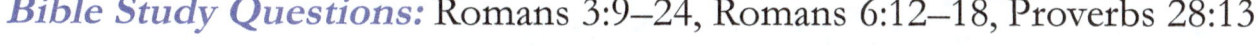

_____

_____

_____

_____

_____

2. According to Romans 3:22–24, how do we become right before God?

_____

_____

_____

_____

_____

3. Reflecting on Romans 6:12–18, should sin control our lives?

_____

_____

_____

_____

_____

4. How do we experience freedom from sin?

_____

_____

_____

_____

5. What does Proverbs 28:13 say about sin?

_____

_____

_____

_____

_____

Words from the Author

Sin, as you know, is not a character trait that has to be taught, but it is embedded in our DNA. As my wife and I began raising a family, this became evident. Our

sons Joshua and Hunter clearly showed that rebellion starts very young. As my wife and I started having children, we were amazed at how defiant even young toddlers can be. It's like when we would tell them no, they would go out of their way to do it.

Unfortunately, every human has involuntarily inherited this sin problem from Adam and Eve, our ancestors. God made it clear that Adam and Eve had free rein within the beautiful garden created for them to live, except for one particular tree. The tree of knowledge of good and evil was off-limits, and God instructed that if they ate its fruit, they would die. Similar to my personal experience of telling our toddlers no, Eve finds herself drawn to the one tree to which God says no. Satan uses his extraordinary deceptive nature to convince Eve that this will be a great experience without the consequences of death. Not only did Eve eat the fruit, but Adam as well, and as a result of that first sin, death came just as God had proclaimed. Not only was death the result of sin, but separation as well. Adam and Eve were evicted from paradise and their daily walk with God. The only antidote for the sin problem would be an unblemished sacrifice offered by God. The only sacrifice that would qualify was God's only son.

Jesus came to the earth to restore the fellowship between humanity and God, which was cut off thousands of years prior. As a result of His death, burial, and resurrection, redemption is now available to all humanity. Jesus took our sin upon Himself so that we could become the righteousness of God. The simple act of believing that Jesus is the son of God and inviting Him into your life gives us the right to become heirs of God and co-heirs with Jesus. The

beauty of this redemptive process is that now we are in right standing with God and have been granted access to His eternal kingdom.

By accepting this gift of Christ, our sins are forgiven, our failures forgotten, and we become new people in Christ. This doesn't mean that you will never sin again, but that sin will not rule your life. Sin has lost control, and the power of Jesus is now governing our life. At this conversion's point, a rebirth takes place that is difficult to explain. Some people experience a dramatic emotional feeling at this point while others have a more inward change. You are now a new creature; old things have passed away, and new things are on the horizon.

Personally, I've had several encounters with the Lord. When I was a younger child around eight years old, I remember having a love for God and a desire to please Him. Then as I became a teenager, I drifted away from Him. At around sixteen years old, my younger brother Steve and I were feeding the cattle hay after dark when a strong feeling came over me to pray and ask for salvation. My brother and I both prayed and felt great and even shared the experience with family members. I began reading the Bible for several weeks and praying, but found myself slipping back to the old ways.

During the next six years, I would completely fall away and live a life not pleasing to God. The best thing that happened to me during this time was meeting Connie Kerr, a beautiful young lady I fell in love with who cared deeply for me. Five years later, Connie became my beautiful bride, and we began living life outside the blessings of a Godly marriage. The great thing was that God began stirring my heart and showing

me that I needed God in my life and my marriage. I began spending some time with my older brother Ronnie, who had come to the Lord earlier that year, and he had been sharing with me the need for Jesus.

One day after he and I talked, I was at home outside my house when the Holy Spirit came back to me in a similar way as when I was sixteen. This time I responded with a short but sincere prayer that went something like this: "God, if You will forgive me, I will serve You the rest of my life." That day, after praying that simple prayer, I felt a change in my life. It was like a tremendous weight was lifted off me, and I felt great. I was born again, which was absolutely incredible. I wanted everyone to know what I had experienced and, for the life of me, couldn't understand why anyone wouldn't want this.

Looking back, I'm sure I was slightly overzealous about my conversion. I was employed at a large plastic factory in Knoxville, Tennessee, and within several months, I had made it a point to speak with every person working on my shift about their need to be saved. The astonishing thing was that everyone except one told me they were already saved. I later realized that these men were telling me they were saved to get me off their backs. I didn't see one salvation, but it wasn't because of a lack of zeal. I later understood that if I sowed the seed, another would come along, and water and God would give the increase. The greatest feeling I've experienced is knowing I'm forgiven and accepted into God's family. This journey started thirty-five years ago, and I have never been the same!

Reading Study Question

1. Where did sin originate? How was it passed along to you?

   _____

   _____

   _____

   _____

   _____

2. Have you noticed the sinful nature in a child? Explain.

   _____

   _____

   _____

   _____

   _____

3. Why do you feel we are drawn to things we can't have?

_____

_____

_____

_____

_____

4. What were the results of Adam and Eve eating from the forbidden tree?

_____

_____

_____

_____

_____

5. Explain the impact sin has in our life.

_____

_____

_____

_____

_____

6. What role did Jesus play in restoring our fellowship with God?

_____

_____

_____

_____

_____

7. Explain the process of being born again and receiving Jesus as savior.

   _____

   _____

   _____

   _____

   _____

8. In a group setting, share your conversion experience.

   _____

   _____

   _____

   _____

   _____

9. What role do you play in seeing people come to Christ?

   _____

   _____

   _____

   _____

   _____

CHAPTER 12: GRACE = ADOPTION

Bible Study Verses: 2 Samuel 9, Galatians 4:4–7
Memory Verse:

> A father to the fatherless, a defender of widows, is God in his holy dwelling. (Psalm 68:5 NIV)

Background

One of the most beautiful acts of service one can do is to adopt a child and make them rightful heirs of the family. This is precisely what God did when He invited us into the family of God. He adopted us and made us joint heirs with Christ. In this chapter, we'll better understand Christ's love for us.

Memory Verse Question

1. Name some ways an orphan could be at a disadvantage.

    _____

    _____

    _____

2. What does God say about the fatherless in our memory verse?

    _____

    _____

    _____

3. What are some scenarios that would leave a child an orphan?

    _____

    _____

    _____

4. Do you feel the Church has any responsibility in helping the orphans? If yes, what can the Church do?

_____

_____

_____

5. Name some people in the Bible who received care, training, and mentorship from someone other than their biological parents.

_____

_____

_____

Bible Study Questions: 2 Samuel 9, Galatians 4:4–7

1. Who was Mephibosheth, mentioned in 2 Samuel chapter 9?

_____

_____

_____

_____

_____

2. What was the name of the man who he lived with in Lodebar, and what do we know about him?

_____

_____

_____

_____

_____

3. How was Mephibosheth welcomed into David's house?

_____

_____

_____

_____

_____

4. Why did David show Mephibosheth so much love?

_____

_____

_____

_____

_____

5. Explain how it feels knowing you have a seat at the King's table.

_____

_____

_____

_____

_____

6. According to Galatians 4:4–7, why did God send His son?

_____

_____

_____

_____

_____

7. In your own words, explain what it means to be an heir of God.

_____

_____

_____

_____

_____

Words from the Author

Every person is born with a desire to be part of a family. Unfortunately, there are some cases where children are not wanted by their biological parents, and they turn to abortion. If you have had an abortion or helped assist someone else with one, I want you to know that there is no condemnation in Christ. As we discussed in the previous chapter, all have sinned and fallen short of the glory of God. Recently the Supreme Court of the United States of America overturned Roe v. Wade, a 1971–1973 landmark decision that ruled that a state law that banned abortion was unconstitutional. This ruling by the Supreme Court was an answered prayer and a victory for the unborn child.

As believers, we must encourage foster care and adoption. Some extended family members occasionally adopt these children, but they are often turned over to state custody. I have adult friends who have shared horrific stories of being abandoned as children, which resulted in tremendous stress and pain from the feeling of not being wanted. A member of our church staff shared a story of being taken from his parents and placed in state custody at nine years old. He recalls the night the police came to his house and had to remove him and his

> "I did nothing to deserve God's love; in fact, I was living as an orphan, without hope. Yet God chose to pursue a relationship with me, and through the death of his son Jesus, I was adopted into God's family."
>
> —Steven Curtis Chapman—

siblings from a dangerous environment of neglect. While sitting in the back seat of a police cruiser, looking out of the window, he recalls the deep pain he felt as the car pulled out of the family driveway. Little did he know that he would never live with his biological family again. Later, a Godly Christian family decided to adopt him and his siblings and provide an atmosphere of love and stability. Today that same person has some incredible accomplishments, such as graduating college, starting a fam-

ily, and leading a thriving ministry serving as children's pastor. I don't think it's coincidental that this young man not only has three biological children of his own, but recently adopted two more children; what an extraordinary illustration of the impact adoption has had on one child.

Now think about yourself for a minute. Were you not in need of adoption? Was there not a time when you felt alone and needed a Heavenly Father? As we addressed in the previous chapter, because of Adam's fall, we were separated from our Father, and the only way of reconciliation was to be adopted. Grace became the driving force of this adoption process. Grace is unmerited favor, or in other words, it's God's love and mercy given unconditionally. When we experience this type of acceptance and love, it naturally becomes a reciprocating process. We are enthusiastic about sharing with others when we have a positive experience, such as discovering a good restaurant or seeing a great movie.

Understanding that the entire human race has an invisible desire to be part of a healthy family atmosphere is key to knowing how to approach unbelievers with the gospel. Our initial conversations with unchurched people should be coated with grace and shared without condemnation. Grace opens the door to people's hearts, allowing the adoption process to begin. Just as the adoption process for children can be a challenge requiring lots of patience, the same goes for the spiritual adoption process, and we must be persistent but patient. Being adopted into the family of God has extraordinary benefits. One of the benefits is receiving an eternal home in heaven, which is inconceivable. There are numer-

ous passages in the Bible concerning our heavenly dwelling, but there are also lots of scriptures referencing the benefits we have while living here on earth. When a person enters the family of God, we use the terminology that they are saved.

Interestingly enough, the Greek word for *saved* is *sozo*, which means "to save, deliver, protect, heal, preserve, do well, and be made whole." As we can see, this adoption process releases a myriad of blessings and benefits. As people accept Christ and come into God's family, we must be prepared to open our arms and welcome them with unconditional love.

Reading Study Question

1. Explain in your own words what adoption means to you.

    _____

    _____

    _____

    _____

    _____

2. Describe how you think a child feels who has no family.

    _____

    _____

    _____

    _____

    _____

3. Name some reasons everyone needs a family.

    _____

    _____

    _____

    _____

    _____

4. Explain how people are adopted into the family of God.

    _____

    _____

    _____

    _____

    _____

5. What is your role in this adoption process?

_____

_____

_____

_____

_____

6. What are some ways the Church can improve this adoption process?

_____

_____

_____

_____

_____

7. How do discipleship and adoption intertwine?

_____

_____

_____

_____

_____

CHAPTER 13: EFFECTIVE WITNESSING

Bible Study Verses: Acts 1:8, 2 Corinthians 5:20, Mark 16:15, 1 Peter 3:15
Memory Verse:

> In the same way, let your light shine before others, so that they may see your good works and give glory to your Father who is in Heaven. (Matthew 5:16 ESV)

Background

The early Church understood the effectiveness of sharing the gospel. Acts 19:10 tells us that all of Asia heard of Jesus in a short period of time as a result of effective witnessing. In this chapter, we will learn more about witnessing.

Memory Verse Questions

1. Describe what it means to let your light shine before others.

    _____

    _____

    _____

2. This passage of Scripture tells us that people are watching our actions. Do actions speak louder than words? Explain.

    _____

    _____

    _____

3. Give some examples of good works.

    _____

    _____

    _____

4. Before you were a Christian, did you watch how Christians lived? What was your observation?

_____

_____

_____

5. Pew Research Center has said that Christianity is no longer the fastest-growing religion, but now it's Islam. What factors do you think contributed to this situation?

_____

_____

_____

Bible Study Questions: Acts 1:8, 2 Corinthians 5:20, Mark 16:15 1, Peter 3:15

1. What did Jesus tell the disciples they would receive when the Holy Spirit comes upon them?

_____

_____

_____

_____

_____

2. Fill in the blank. Effective _____ requires the power of God.

_____

_____

_____

_____

_____

3. Who are we to witness to?

_____

_____

_____

_____

_____

4. Second Corinthians 5:20 tells us we are an ambassador. Explain the role of an ambassador.

_____

_____

_____

_____

_____

5. As ambassadors of Christ, what is our message?

_____

_____

_____

_____

6. Why is it essential that we are always prepared to share this message?

_____

_____

_____

_____

7. Describe what it means to witness with gentleness and respect.

_____

_____

_____

_____

_____

8. Do you find witnessing difficult? Why or why not?

_____

_____

_____

_____

_____

9. What can you do to become a more effective witness?

"Successful witnessing is taking the initiative to share Christ in the power of the Holy Spirit and leaving the results to God."

—Bill Bright—

_____

_____

_____

_____

_____

Words from the Author

Have you ever known someone notorious for stretching the truth? As you read the previous question, I'm sure a name came to your mind. On the flip side, I'm sure you know people who have great integrity and are always truthful. Being an effective witness for Christ should be a goal we all share. Jesus clearly communicated to the disciples that they were to be witnesses not only to those closest to them but to those around the world. We can look back through the lenses of time and see that these disciples were very effective at telling the story. Effective witnessing is done by simply telling your story.

In the courtroom setting, attorneys will coach their witnesses on how to be effective while testifying to the jury. One of the

most important pieces of coaching advice is to act naturally and be yourself. By being natural, your testimony will come across as compelling and believable. We should use this critical witnessing technique when sharing our faith with someone.

Over the years, I've talked with many Christians who have severe struggles with witnessing to someone. The reasons for these struggles vary, but I frequently hear "I don't know the scriptures well enough." or "I'm afraid I won't have the correct answers." Fear is a tactic the enemy places on us to keep us quiet. One of the most effective witnesses in the Bible was the woman that Jesus met at the well. This woman was a Samaritan whom the Jews didn't associate with and would go out of their way to avoid. Not only did Jesus start a conversation with her, but he also began to witness to her.

There's a great lesson here: everyone deserves to hear the gospel or the good news of Jesus. If God places someone in your path, you should view it as an opportunity to share Jesus with them. Notice that Jesus offers this woman a drink of living water and tells her that if she drinks of it, she will never thirst again. A conversation is sparked, and the woman begins asking Jesus questions. Another lesson in effective witnessing is the importance of creating dialogue, which is not a one-way conversation. Asking questions and listening are two fundamental methods often overlooked when witnessing. These methods will make a practical conversation pathway that will result in effective witnessing. The Holy Spirit's role in witnessing is by far the most crucial element that is needed. The Holy Spirit brings the supernatural component that affirms the words you share and gives you the boldness and confidence to speak.

When Jesus asked the woman to bring her husband back to him, she replied, "I have no husband." Notice Jesus agreed with her and continues by sharing that He's aware that she had been married to five other men, and the one she's with now is not her husband. The Holy Spirit will work in supernatural ways that will allow us to win people to Christ. This woman was so touched by this conversation that she felt compelled to go and tell others about her experience with Jesus. This Samaritan woman's story was convincing because not only did the people of her town listen, but they followed her back to Jesus. Never underestimate the power of your story because there's an entire world just waiting to hear it. Let people know what Jesus has done for you and share it enthusiastically. Encourage people to follow you as you lead them to Jesus. You'll be surprised how many will follow if you are willing to lead the way. You do not see yourself as a leader, but God does. Just pray and ask the Holy Spirit to empower you to be a witness for Him, and great things will happen.

Reading Study Question

1. What role do integrity and truthfulness play in the act of witnessing?

    _____

    _____

    _____

    _____

    _____

2. Who are the disciples instructed to witness to?

    _____

    _____

    _____

    _____

    _____

3. Why did Jesus include Samaria when telling the disciples to go into all the world?

    _____

    _____

    _____

    _____

    _____

4. What lesson was Jesus sending to the disciples when they saw Him witnessing to the Samaritan woman?

    _____

    _____

    _____

    _____

    _____

5. Why is it essential to be natural and act yourself when witnessing?

_____

_____

_____

_____

_____

6. Name some reasons people are afraid of sharing their faith.

_____

_____

_____

_____

_____

7. List some challenges you have in regard to witnessing. What can you do to over-come these?

_____

_____

_____

_____

_____

8. Why is listening essential in effective witnessing?

_____

_____

_____

_____

_____

9. What role does the Holy Spirit play in witnessing?

_____

_____

_____

_____

_____

CHAPTER 14: THE TRINITY

Bible Study Verses: Genesis 1:1, 26; 2 Corinthians 13:14; 1 John 5:7–8; Matthew 3:16–17; Matthew 28:19; Deuteronomy 6:4
Memory Verse:

> And the Holy Spirit descended on him in bodily form, like a dove; and a voice came from Heaven, "You are my beloved Son; with you I am well pleased." (Luke 3:22 ESV)

Background

Although the word *Trinity* is not found in the Bible, the concept is established throughout the Scriptures. We will look at the original Hebrew word used for *God* in the first chapter of Genesis and discover how that supports the Trinity.

Memory Verse Questions

1. Name the three deities present at the baptism of Jesus.

   _____

   _____

   _____

2. In what way did the Holy Spirt appear at Jesus's baptism?

   _____

   _____

   _____

3. How did God the Father appear at Jesus's baptism?

   _____

   _____

   _____

4. Why did God the Father, Jesus the son, and the Holy Spirit all need to be present at this event?

_____

_____

_____

5. What, if any, questions do you have regarding Jesus' baptism?

_____

_____

_____

Bible Study Questions: Genesis 1:1, 26; 2 Corinthians 13:14; 1 John 5:7–8; Matthew 3:16–17; Matthew 28:19; Deuteronomy 6:4

1. What is the Hebrew word used for *God* in Genesis 1:1?

_____

_____

_____

_____

_____

2. Why do you suppose *Elohim* is plural?

_____

_____

_____

_____

_____

3. In Genesis 1:26, who was God speaking to when He said, "Let us make man in our own image"?

_____

_____

_____

_____

_____

4. In Paul's prayer in 2 Corinthians 13:14, how do you see him reference the Trinity?

_____

_____

_____

_____

_____

5. What does 1 John 5:7 say about the Father, Son, and the Holy Spirit?

_____

_____

_____

_____

_____

6. What instruction did Jesus give His disciples in Matthew 28:19 regarding baptism?

_____

_____

_____

_____

_____

7. Deuteronomy 6:4 says that there is one God. In your own words, give an illustration of the Trinity.

_____

_____

_____

_____

_____

Words from the Author

Have you ever been associated with someone who, regardless of the conversation topic, always seemed to know something about it? I worked with a fellow employee who seemed to know everything and wasn't shy about telling you. Unfortunately, he acquired the reputation of being a know-it-all, or at least thinking he did.

Before you begin to read my thoughts on the Trinity, understand that I don't claim to possess a complete exegesis on this subject. When explaining one God in three persons, I must confess that it can be puzzling. A human being cannot fully understand and describe God because the Scripture tells us His ways are much higher than ours. It would be like a lump of clay explaining the details of the potter. That would be impossible, but one thing we can see is the potter's character through the work of his vessels. We can better understand God and His character through His creation. For example, when you look at His creative work, such as the universe and all the planets, you see that God is very methodical and creates with extreme detail. When I see the sun and moon, it reminds me that nothing was made out of random actions, but everything created was intentional and has a significant purpose.

We see in Genesis 1:1 that the Hebrew word used for *God* is *Elohim*, which is plural. So this enlightens us on the fact that God wasn't alone in the work of His creation. In verse 26 of the same chapter, we see the creation of man. Notice that God speaks to the Holy Trinity when He says, "Let us make man in our own image." At this point, we are introduced to the tripartite of God. *God the Father*, which we hear from here in Genesis 1: *Jesus the Son who is the Word of God*; and *the Holy Spirit*, which hovers over the deep in Genesis 1:2. Concerning being created in God's image, notice that man has a tripartite as well, that being body, soul, and spirit. Notice that only man was designed with these three parts of all the creations, including all the animals. Just as the vessel reflects the potter, man's and woman's formation is a reflection of God. The Scripture references the three parts of man:

> May God himself, the God of peace, sanctify you through and through. May your whole spirit, soul and body be kept blameless at the coming of our Lord Jesus Christ. (1 Thessalonians 5:23 NIV)

In his prayer, Paul addresses all three parts of our human makeup. God likewise reveals Himself in three parts: the Father, Son, and the Holy Spirit. Interesting that the Trinity is always in unison and inseparable in purpose. Let me illustrate this way: If you hold an egg in your hand, you are actually holding the shell, yolk, and the white. In describing to someone what's in your hand, you would never say I'm holding a shell in my hand unless the egg was separated. The triune God can never be separated on purpose; that is why you hear Jesus say, "When you've seen Me, you've seen the Father." The three are one and unified in total agreement. Scripture describes the

current setting of the Godhead as God the Father sitting on the throne with Jesus the Son sitting at His right hand and the Holy Spirit dwelling within believers here on planet earth. Jesus is positioned at the right hand of the Father, serving as our advocate. An advocate is a person who speaks or writes in defense of another. We see this role carried out in the court of law when a lawyer speaks on behalf of a defendant. Jesus also serves as our intercessor, which intervenes for us. It's incredibly comforting knowing that even though sin separated us from God, the Holy Spirit brought us to a knowledge of the redemptive work of Jesus Christ. Because of this, all humanity can be saved and restored.

Reading Study Questions

1. Describe why it's difficult to comprehend the entire nature of God.

_____

_____

_____

_____

_____

2. How can we better understand the nature of God?

_____

_____

_____

_____

3. Explain how you came to the conclusion that God was not alone during the creation process.

_____

_____

_____

_____

_____

4. Name the three that make up the Godhead.

   _____

   _____

   _____

   _____

   _____

5. What are the three parts of the human makeup?

   _____

   _____

   _____

   _____

   _____

6. Explain why the Trinity is inseparable.

   _____

   _____

   _____

   _____

   _____

7. Based on your understanding, describe each role of the Godhead.

   ➢ God the Father

   _____

   _____

   _____

   _____

   _____

➤ Jesus

_____

_____

_____

_____

_____

➤ The Holy Spirit

_____

_____

_____

_____

_____

8. What role does Jesus and the Holy Spirit play in man's restoration with God the Father?

_____

_____

_____

_____

_____

OUR BAPTISMS

The Greek word for *baptize* is *bapitizo*, meaning "to be submerged or cleansed by dipping." Three baptisms are clearly defined in the new covenant and are essential to our spiritual growth. In the following chapters, we will examine each baptism and discover its significant purpose.

CHAPTER 15: BAPTISM IN SALVATION

Bible Study Verses: Acts 2:14–41, 1 Corinthians 12:13, 1 Peter 3:21, John 3:18–19

Memory Verse:

> And when he comes, he will convict the world concerning sin and righteousness and judgment. (John 16:8 ESV)

Background

The phrase "baptism in salvation" is not a common expression heard often. In this chapter, we will explore the meaning of baptism and learn what role the Holy Spirit serves in the process of salvation.

Memory Verse Questions

1. In the memory verse, who is Jesus referring to as the one who is coming?

   _____

   _____

   _____

2. Describe what it means to convict the world of sin.

   _____

   _____

   _____

3. Have you experienced the conviction of the Holy Spirit in your life? If so, give an example.

   _____

   _____

   _____

4. What role does the Holy Spirit play in someone becoming a follower of Christ?

_____

_____

_____

5. Explain how you should pray for unbelievers regarding the work of the Holy Spirit.

_____

_____

_____

6. What are some signs that the Holy Spirit is convicting an unbeliever? What role can you play in this process?

_____

_____

_____

_____

_____

7. The Holy Spirit convinces nonbelievers of their sin and need for Christ. Does this convicting work continue after salvation? Explain.

_____

_____

_____

_____

_____

Bible Study Questions: Acts 2:14–41, 1 Corinthians 12:13, 1 Peter 3:21, John 3:18–19

1. Explain the difference in Peter before and after the upper room experience.

   _____

   _____

   _____

   _____

   _____

2. Describe the reaction of the people in Acts 2:37.

   _____

   _____

   _____

   _____

> "Through salvation our past has been forgiven, our present is given meaning, and our future is secured."
>
> —Rick Warren—

   _____

3. What is the meaning of "they were cut to the heart"?

   _____

   _____

   _____

   _____

   _____

4. The question was asked by the people: "What shall we do?" Explain Peter's response.

   _____

   _____

   _____

   _____

   _____

5. In 1 Corinthians 12:3, Paul said no one can say "Jesus is Lord" except by the Holy Spirit. In your own words, explain this.

_____

_____

_____

_____

_____

6. When baptism is mentioned, often the initial thought is water baptism. In 1 Corinthians 12:13, Paul is not speaking of water baptism, but a baptism into the body. Who administers the baptism into the Body of Christ?

_____

_____

_____

_____

_____

7. According to 1 Corinthians 12:13, explain how the Holy Spirit eliminates all racial divides concerning the Body of Christ.

_____

_____

_____

_____

_____

8. In your own words, explain 1 Peter 3:21.

_____

_____

_____

_____

_____

Words from the Author

Becoming a born-again follower of Christ is the single most important decision you will ever make. Words can't adequately describe just how wonderful it is to be part of the Body of Christ. As I write this book, I think of all the followers of Christ I've had the privilege of meeting over the years. From the most remote areas of Zambia to the northern parts of Kenya, I've had the opportunity to see the Body of Christ in action across Africa. I've visited churches in South America from Mexico to Chile and have witnessed the Body of Christ alive and well. Regardless of your physical location, if you're born again, you're a member of the Body of Christ and have a great assignment. The Bible teaches to become a follower of Jesus that the Holy Spirit must draw you to the point of decision. A person cannot experience salvation without this inner work.

John 15:16 explains, "You did not choose me, but *I chose you* and appointed you so that you might go and bear fruit—fruit that will last—and so that whatever you ask in my name, the Father will give you." Passages such as this reiterate that the Holy Spirit is at work before an individual accepts Christ and become a follower of Him. An extraordinary thing happens when a lost person adheres to the drawing power of the Holy Spirit. An inward transformation occurs as the Holy Spirit baptizes that individual into the Body of Christ.

> I will give you *a new heart* and put a new spirit in you; *I will remove from you your heart of stone and give you a heart of flesh.* (Ezekiel 36:26 NIV)

It's an inward work that will result in an outward change. Our hard hearts become pliable through this incredible experience. This transformation can be compared to the phenomenon of a caterpillar changing into a butterfly called metamorphosis. Just as the butterfly is changed forever, we continue to be changed forever through this spiritual metamorphosis. The trigger that begins this spiritual process is confessing Jesus as your personal Lord and savior.

> If you declare with your mouth, *"Jesus is Lord,"* and believe in your heart that God raised him from the dead, you will be saved. (Romans 10:9 NIV)

This transformation begins in the heart and flows outward. Religion emphasizes learning the rules and keeping them, which tends to create what I call a transformational reversal. A transformational reversal creates change, but in reverse. When our focus is on changing people outwardly, we run the risk of individuals never being saved. Jesus often addressed this issue during his ministry and referred to it as hypocrisy. He used an illustration of the Scribes and Pharisees to expose their pretense by saying, "You clean the outside of the cup, but inside, you are filthy." These guys knew all the rules and regulations but hadn't experienced a heart change.

Barna Research Group has determined that more than 50 percent of people in

the American Church are confused about their salvation. Barna Research Group also revealed that 44 percent of Americans are "notional Christians." These ninety million notional Christians are people who describe themselves as Christians but do not believe that their hope for eternal life is based on a personal relationship with Jesus and the belief that He died and rose again from the dead. This is an alarming statistic when you consider how many people attending the American Church have missed out on the main point of being saved! Every Church needs a very intentional discipleship model to ensure these fundamental teachings are intact.

Reading Study Questions

1. What is the single most important decision you will ever make?

   _____

   _____

   _____

   _____

   _____

2. How do you become a member of the Body of Christ? What role does the Holy Spirit play in this process?

   _____

   _____

   _____

   _____

   _____

3. What changes can someone expect after receiving Jesus as Lord and Savior?

   _____

   _____

   _____

   _____

   _____

4. What is the transformation process of a caterpillar to a butterfly called? How is this similar to the born-again experience?

_____

_____

_____

_____

_____

5. What is the trigger that begins the spiritual transformation?

_____

_____

_____

_____

_____

6. Explain transformational reversal.

_____

_____

_____

_____

_____

7. How did Jesus respond to the Scribes and Pharisees regarding their outward appearance?

_____

_____

_____

_____

_____

8. Why do you think so many people are confused about their salvation?

_____

_____

_____

_____

_____

9. What is needed to ensure that these fundamental teachings are intact?

_____

_____

_____

_____

_____

CHAPTER 16: BAPTISM IN WATER

Bible Study Verses: Matthew 3:16, Matthew 28:19, Colossians 2:12–14
Memory Verse:

> We were therefore buried with him through baptism into death in order that, just as Christ was raised from the dead through the glory of the Father, we too may live a new life. (Romans 6:4 NIV)

Background

Jesus left two ordinances for the Church to administer: communion and water baptism. This chapter will address the significance of water baptism and its purpose in a believer's life.

Memory Verse Questions

1. What do you think Paul spoke of when he metaphorically said we had been buried with Christ?

   _____

   _____

   _____

2. Since death to self comes at salvation, what process signifies the burial?

   _____

   _____

   _____

3. Why do you think Paul associated baptism with living a new life?

   _____

   _____

   _____

4. Is this new life contingent on following Christ in water baptism?

_____

_____

_____

5. Explain the significance in Matthew 28:19, where Jesus said, "Go make disciples, baptizing them in the name of the Father, Son, and Holy Spirit." Why are discipleship and baptism linked?

_____

_____

_____

6. In your own words, describe the importance of water baptism.

_____

_____

_____

Bible Study Questions: Matthew 3:16, Matthew 28:19, Colossians 2:12–14

1. Who baptized Jesus?

_____

_____

_____

_____

_____

2. Where did Jesus's baptism take place?

_____

_____

_____

_____

_____

3. Explain the presence of the Trinity at Jesus's baptism.

_____

_____

_____

_____

_____

4. Since Jesus was perfect without sin, why was He baptized?

_____

_____

_____

_____

_____

5. Jesus always led by example, such as in water baptism. Name some ways we can lead by example.

_____

_____

_____

_____

_____

6. Who was Jesus talking to in Matthew 28:19? Is this command for you as well?

_____

_____

_____

_____

_____

7. Explain what it means to come alive in Christ.

_____

_____

_____

_____

_____

8. Explain how it feels to have your debt erased.

_____

_____

_____

_____

_____

Words from the Author

For several years after my conversion, I questioned deep and long whether I should be baptized again. Being raised in the Church, it was common for children to be baptized at a young age. I still recall going forward several times as a young boy, especially if the message had anything to do with hell. What young boy wouldn't choose heaven over hell—that was a no-brainer! Reflecting back, my problem was that I didn't understand salvation until later in life. As a young boy, I was baptized in water, but didn't fully realize water baptism's purpose or significance.

John the Baptist was the first person mentioned in the Bible to baptize people in water. John is known as the forerunner of Jesus and was also a first cousin of Jesus.

> "Baptism was to put a line of demarcation between your past sins when you are buried with Him by Baptism - you are burying your past sins - eradicating them - putting a line in the sand saying that old man is dead and he is no longer alive anymore and I rise up to walk in the newness of life."
>
> —T.D. Jakes—

He referred to himself in John 1:23 (ESV): He said, "I am the voice of one crying out in the wilderness, 'Make straight the way of the Lord,' as the prophet Isaiah said." He was announcing the coming of the Messiah, whose message was "repent, for

the kingdom of God is at hand." John is arguably one of the most well-known men in the Bible. John's appearance was also pre-announced in Isaiah 40:3–5, showing God's significant purpose for his ministry.

His dress and evangelistic style were very different from the religious people of his day. John wore clothing made of camel's hair with a distinctive leather belt around his waist. Interestingly, his diet consisted of locusts and wild honey, which corresponded with his rugged appearance. John's life was purposefully simple, focusing primarily on the kingdom of God. As he continued preaching the message of repentance, his ministry began to experience extraordinary growth. People were drawn to him and his convicting message. Many would travel from Jerusalem and even the remote areas of Judea to listen and be baptized.

One day as John was at the River Jordan baptizing the people, Jesus appeared and asked John to baptize Him. John's initial response was, "You should baptize me," but Jesus insisted that it was necessary to fulfill all righteousness. It wasn't that Jesus needed to repent because, as we know, He was sinless, but He was leading by example and showing the significance of water baptism. Water baptism doesn't save you, but it should follow salvation. When someone is drawn by the Holy Spirit and receives Christ, a supernatural miracle occurs. The human nature (old man) dies, and the new man (new creature) comes alive, which is the first step a lost person must take. Jesus clearly laid out the next step, water baptism, and at this point, another phenomenon happens: the old person or human nature is buried. At this point, you are detached from the old way of living and show the world your new way of life.

On one occasion, I was performing a water baptism in a local river called the Little River. I'll never forget the setting as a small group of men from our Church wanted to be baptized after Church on a Wednesday evening. We left the Church and traveled maybe ten minutes down to a swimming hole at the river. When we arrived, two groups of people were on the riverbank, and both were drinking beer. We asked if it was okay if we used the area for just a few minutes to baptize some new believers. The first group said they were about to leave, packed their beer, and left. The second group decided to stay and watch. As our small group of men, maybe twenty or so, gathered in the shallow water and began with a prayer, I then walked out into the deeper water, and one by one, I baptized the men in the name of the Father, the Son, and the Holy Spirit. I noticed the men who were drinking on the bank were paying close attention.

As I finished baptizing the men from our Church, I saw some movement up on the bank. I noticed a big man in his sixties standing up and looking around. Then what came next caught me by surprise. He began pulling his shirt off and walking down the bank toward the river. I didn't know if he was upset that we had taken too long, but he was making his way toward me. As he walked through the water, maybe fifty yards off the shore, he kept getting bigger the closer he came. He was a very rough-looking man with a weathered face and long hair. As he approached, I noticed tears running down his face as he asked me if I would baptize him. I shared with him that if he confessed

his sins and believed in Jesus, he would be saved. He dropped his head and began to weep no longer than I said those words. I baptized that man, and he came out of the water with a glow on his face. The joy of the Lord had come on him. I was so excited at what had just happened that I didn't see what was coming next. Another man had come off the bank and was now ready to be baptized! Two men drinking beer and enjoying their evening saw men being baptized and felt under conviction and were drawn to the river, very similar to the way people were drawn to the Jordan River.

Ryan Watson being baptized by Pastor Pacer and Pastor Oliver at the Little River in Tennessee.

Reading Study Questions

1. Who was the first person in the Bible to baptize others in waters? What was his message?

_____

_____

_____

_____

_____

2. Name some of the ways John differed from the religious leaders of his time.

_____

_____

_____

_____

3. Why do you think people were drawn to John the Baptist?

_____

_____

_____

_____

4. Explain John's response when Jesus asked to be baptized.

_____

_____

_____

_____

5. Describe the significance of water baptism and who should be baptized.

_____

_____

_____

_____

6. Write down your personal baptism experience and the impact it had on you and those around you.

   _____

   _____

   _____

   _____

   _____

CHAPTER 17: BAPTISM IN THE HOLY SPIRIT

Bible Study Verses: Joel 2:28, Isaiah 44:3, Acts 2:15–18, Luke 11:13, John 16:7, Luke 24:49, Acts 1:8, Acts 2:4

Memory Verse:

> I indeed baptize you with water unto repentance, but He who is coming after me is mightier than I, whose sandals I am not worthy to carry. He will baptize you with the Holy Spirit and fire. (Matthew 3:11 NKJV)

Background

Jesus distinctly communicated to His disciples that before they began their ministry, He would send them the promised Holy Spirit. In this chapter, we will discover why Jesus placed so much emphasis on being filled with the Holy Spirit and why we need Him today.

Memory Verse Questions

1. What was John's relation to Jesus?

   _____

   _____

   _____

2. John the Baptist was a very popular person throughout the Roman Empire. How did he view himself in comparison to Jesus?

   _____

   _____

   _____

3. What was the proclamation that John made concerning Jesus?

   _____

   _____

   _____

4. How many people did Jesus baptize in water?

_____

_____

_____

5. Why do you think Jesus left the role of water baptism up to His disciples?

_____

_____

_____

6. Explain in your own words what it means to be baptized with the Holy Spirit and fire.

_____

_____

_____

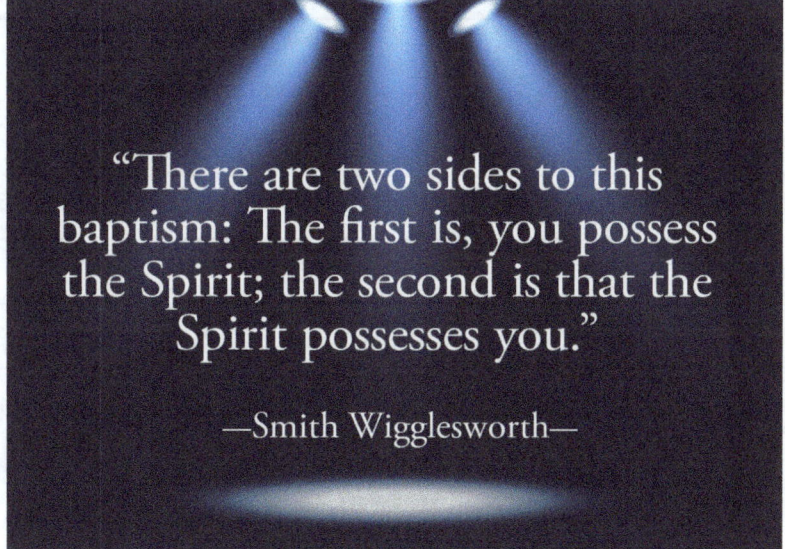

"There are two sides to this baptism: The first is, you possess the Spirit; the second is that the Spirit possesses you."

—Smith Wigglesworth—

Bible Study Questions: Joel 2:28, Isaiah 44:3, Acts 2:15–18, Luke 11:13, John 16:7, Luke 24:49, Acts 1:8, Acts 2:4

1. Where in Scripture do you see the prophecy in Joel 2:28 and Isaiah 44:3 being fulfilled?

    _____

    _____

    _____

    _____

    _____

2. Explain Peter's response to the people according to Acts 2:15–16.

    _____

    _____

    _____

    _____

    _____

3. Who is eligible to receive the Holy Spirit according to Luke 11:13?

    _____

    _____

    _____

    _____

    _____

4. Who did Jesus promise to send when He went away (John 16:7)?

    _____

    _____

    _____

    _____

    _____

5. Where did Jesus tell the disciples to go while waiting on the arrival of the Holy Spirit (Luke 24:49)?

_____

_____

_____

_____

_____

6. What did Jesus say would happen when the Holy Spirit comes upon them? (Acts 1:8)

_____

_____

_____

_____

_____

7. What was the reaction as the disciples were filled with the Holy Spirit?

_____

_____

_____

_____

_____

Words from the Author

It's difficult to imagine how the disciples must have felt knowing that Jesus would be leaving them soon. The relationships formed during this time would be an eternal bond. Watching Jesus love the unlovable, heal the sick, and cast out demons must have been remarkable, to say the least. Jesus had shared with the disciples that he must return to the Father, but that didn't make it any easier for these men who left everything to follow Jesus. Leading up to the betrayal and crucifixion, Jesus gave final instructions to His disciples regarding what they could expect after the ascension. One of His comments was that it would be to their advantage for Him to leave because He would send the Holy Spirit back to them. I'm sure the disciples were question-

ing how this could be to their advantage. Jesus, the one whom the winds obeyed and who raised the dead, was leaving them and sending something better? What could be better? Jesus told them that the Holy Spirit would not only be with them, but would live inside them, and He would be their comforter and guide.

Jesus made it clear that they were not ready to embark on their mission, but needed to wait in the city of Jerusalem for the promised Holy Spirit. He also emphasized that they would receive power from the Holy Spirit to be effective witnesses. After Jesus gave His final words to the disciples, He ascended out of sight. At this point, 120 disciples obeyed His words and assembled in Jerusalem, waiting for the promise that Jesus had spoken would come to pass. It was a hectic time in Jerusalem as Jews and God-fearing people were traveling from all over the world to celebrate the Feast of Pentecost. I'm sure it wasn't easy to find a place to stay, but the disciples had arranged to stay in the upper room.

During the next ten days, I'm confident the 120 relived the previous three years, sharing their account of what had transpired in the life of Jesus. I'm sure Peter, James, and John went into detail about some of their experiences, such as the mountain of transfiguration when Moses and Elijah appeared with Jesus. I'm sure there were lots of praying and singing as the anticipation of the Holy Spirit grew stronger. Then day 10 came! Fifty days from Passover on the Day of Pentecost, the disciples were in one mind and one accord when a mighty rushing wind swept through the upper room. I'm sure it was an indescribable moment as all of the men and women in

the room began being filled with the third person of the Godhead. It was like flames of fire landing upon each one of them as they were filled with the Holy Spirit. It was more than the natural body could absorb as they seemed as if they were drunk on wine, and each spoke in languages they had never spoken before!

Peter stood and explained to the crowd that these people were not drunk on wine, but filled with the Holy Spirit. He described what was happening was the prophecy of Joel 2:28 coming to pass before their very eyes. As Peter stood and spoke to the multitude that day, an incredible boldness came upon him. What Jesus said would happen after being filled with the Holy Spirit was happening before their eyes. The anointing was so strong on Peter that three thousand people responded and became followers of Christ. All of these men and women were now empowered with an extraordinary ability to share the gospel of Jesus Christ.

As Peter spoke to the crowd, he mentioned that this experience of being filled with the Holy Spirit was not just for a select few. Peter explained that this promise was for all of them, not just those listening but for their children and their descendants, as many as He would call. Throughout the book of Acts, speaking in an unknown tongue is the most common sign of the initial infilling of the Holy Spirit. I find this intriguing since we know that the tongue is the one member that Paul speaks of as being untamable. Amazing—what man can't do, God can! Paul clearly explained how the gift of tongues should be used in a church setting (1 Corinthians 14). The greatest asset we have as Christ's followers is the Holy Spirit's working. If we are serious about being dis-

ciples of Jesus and desire more of Him, He will baptize us with the Holy Spirit and fire! Notice the difference in Peter before and after he was filled with the Holy Spirit. He becomes an incredible witness for Jesus and speaks with an unusual boldness.

I've noticed that confidence when speaking publicly since I've been filled with the Spirit. Growing up, I was reticent and reserved, especially in a crowd. I met this girl Connie in high school, who was just the opposite of me in terms of quietness. She was the captain of the cheerleading team and voted the friendliest of our senior class. Connie eventually became my wife and helped me come out of my shell. Little did I know that later in life, God would save me, fill me with the Holy Spirit, and call me to pastor an incredible church. I often asked God if He was sure I was the right guy. I didn't understand that every time I stood to speak publicly or to individuals about Jesus, I would receive an anointing from the Holy Spirit to speak with boldness. It's nothing shy of a modern-day miracle to think back on that quiet young boy now standing weekly to talk to several thousand people about Jesus. That only happens through the infilling of the Holy Spirit!

Reading Study Questions

1. Explain how you think the disciples felt when Jesus said He must go away.

   _____

   _____

   _____

   _____

   _____

2. What benefit did Jesus say there would be as a result of Him leaving?

   _____

   _____

   _____

   _____

3. How many days after Passover before the Holy Spirit came? How many days after Jesus's ascension?

_____

_____

_____

_____

_____

4. How many gathered in the upper room, waiting for the promise?

_____

_____

_____

_____

_____

5. Describe the atmosphere when the Holy Spirit made His appearance in the upper room.

_____

_____

_____

_____

_____

6. What did Peter say to the crowds in terms of how these disciples were behaving?

_____

_____

_____

_____

_____

7. Describe the difference you see in Peter before and after he is filled with the Holy Spirit.

_____

_____

_____

_____

_____

8. Do you know anyone who has been filled with the Holy Spirit? If so, explain the before and after.

_____

_____

_____

_____

_____

CHAPTER 18: BEING LED BY THE SPIRIT

Bible Study Verses: Exodus 13:21–22, John 16:13–15, Matthew 4:1, Romans 8:23–27
Memory Verse:

> For all who are led by the Spirit of God are sons of God. (Romans 8:14 ESV)

Background

The Holy Spirit knows what your future holds and will always lead you toward your amazing destiny. This chapter will address how to effectively communicate with the Holy Spirit.

Memory Verse Questions

1. Have you ever been on any type of guided tour? If so, explain the guide's role.

   _____

   _____

   _____

2. Describe in your words what it means to be a son of God.

   _____

   _____

   _____

3. Why do you think Paul uses the correlation of being led by the Spirit with being a son of God?

   _____

   _____

   _____

4. Explain how you have experienced the leading of the Holy Spirit.

_____

_____

_____

5. Do you think the Holy Spirit would ever lead you away from God's perfect will? Why or why not?

_____

_____

_____

6. Describe an occasion when you didn't follow the Holy Spirit and share the outcome.

_____

_____

_____

7. Describe a time when you followed the leading of the Holy Spirit when it didn't make sense.

_____

_____

_____

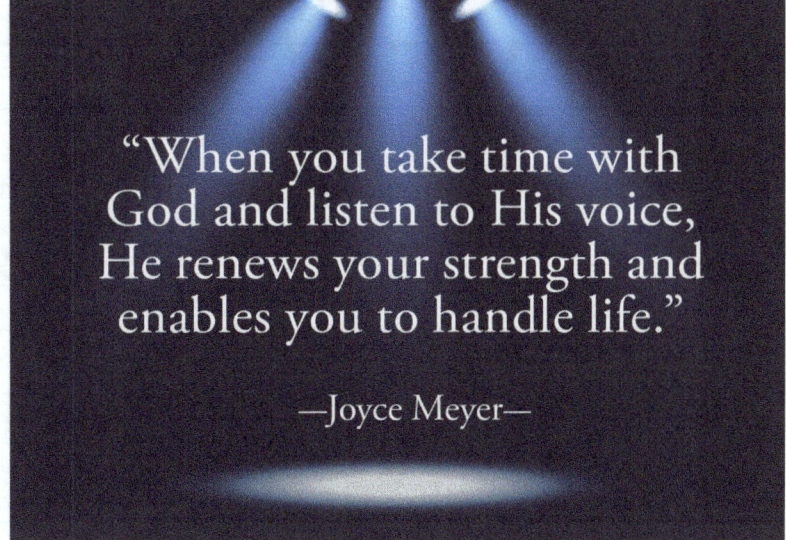

"When you take time with God and listen to His voice, He renews your strength and enables you to handle life."

—Joyce Meyer—

Bible Study Questions: Exodus 13:21–22, John 16:13–15,
Matthew 4:1, Romans 8:23–27

1. According to Exodus 13, what method did God use to guide the Israelites through the desert?

   _____

   _____

   _____

   _____

   _____

2. What statement do you think it sent to Israel knowing God was leading them?

   _____

   _____

   _____

   _____

   _____

3. In John 16, Jesus explains that the Holy Spirit will come after He leaves and will be a guide. In what ways did Jesus say He would guide us?

   _____

   _____

   _____

   _____

   _____

4. Describe what the Holy Spirit would be telling them about the future.

   _____

   _____

   _____

   _____

   _____

5. Who does the Holy Spirit glorify?

_____

_____

_____

_____

6. According to Matthew 4:1, who led Jesus into the wilderness?

_____

_____

_____

_____

_____

7. Romans 8 speaks of the Spirit within us eagerly awaiting an event. What is the occasion we are anticipating?

_____

_____

_____

_____

8. How does the Holy Spirit help us when we don't know what to pray?

_____

_____

_____

_____

9. Explain how the Holy Spirit helps us align with God's will.

_____

_____

_____

_____

_____

Words from the Author

Growing up in a rural area in East Tennessee when the economy wasn't exactly prodigious, finding work as a teenager was difficult. My first official employment would be considered a dream job for most teenage boys. I'll never forget my first day at work for Cades Cove Riding Stables. Hugh and Verna Lee Myers took a risk hiring a fifteen-year-old boy on summer break as a trail guide for their family business. My primary responsibility would be leading a group of horseback riders along trails in the Great Smoky National Park. My secondary role, which I didn't care for that much, was scooping poop out of the stables. Hey, you must take the good with the bad, and the good far outweighed the bad.

My responsibility as a trail guide was leading the group on the correct trails, communicating, and watching out for their safety. During my two summers working as a guide, I only had two incidents, which didn't seem like a lot for a fifteen-to-sixteen-year-old rambunctious boy. The first episode happened as I led a group of about six or seven people. A young boy, maybe five or six

years old, was riding, and I was leading him by a rope attached to my saddle. Around the halfway mark of the one-hour ride, I found

> "The work of the Spirit is to impart life, to implant hope, to give liberty, to testify of Christ, to guide us into all truth, to teach us all things, to comfort the believer, and to convict the world of sin."
>
> —Dwight L. Moody—

myself fighting sleep. The horses knew the trails very well because they were on them practically every day, so my horse was basically on cruise control until I fell asleep and my saddle slid off! I'm sure you're thinking, How could someone doze off while riding a horse? Well, I did, and the problem had just begun as my foot had gotten hung up in the stirrup, and the horse didn't slow down. The only positive thing about the whole event was that the horse didn't run, but continued walking very slowly. I remember each time

I would reach forward to try and release my boot, the horse would take another step, and I would fall backward. This had to be one of the most embarrassing times of my life, and as I sit here and write, believe me, I'm questioning my sanity. To add insult to injury, I'll never forget the words that came out of the little boy's mouth that I was leading. "Momma, Momma, the guide fell off his horse."

Finally, the episode ended when one of the riders got off his horse and came to my rescue by walking up and stopping my horse. When the group of people saw that I was all right, they burst into laughter, and I, in a very composed way, straightened my saddle and continued the ride. Unlike my previous illustration of a guide falling asleep, the Holy Spirit never sleeps or slumbers. He is constantly watching out for our well-being and leading us in the right direction. Like many trails in the Smoky Mountains, there are many paths in life.

To experience life at its best, we need an experienced guide who knows which path to take. Jesus instructed that when He ascended, He would send the Holy Spirit, which would serve as our guide and much more. In the scripture below, you will see the Holy Spirit referred to as "helper."

And I will pray the Father, and He will give you another Helper, that He may abide with you forever—the Spirit of truth, whom the world cannot receive, because it neither sees Him nor knows Him; but you know Him, for He dwells with you and will be in you. (John 14:16–17 NKJV)

The word for *helper* in the original Greek is *parakletos*, meaning "one called to the side of another." The Holy Spirit's role is to lead us in the direction that brings honor and glory to God. Having a daily trainer/guide sent from heaven is an extraordinary advantage in terms of living for Christ and pleasing Him.

A question was asked: what is the greatest challenge that your organization faces in terms of hindering productivity? My answer was communication, or lack thereof. I've found that in any arena, including Church, business, or family, where there is a lack of communication, there tends to be a growing separation between team members. If not solved, this can create frustration and a lack of direction from everyone involved. Could you imagine beginning a new job you're unfamiliar with, receiving no training, or being designated a trainer but never communicating with your trainee? This scenario would leave both parties upset. The Holy Spirit has been appointed our trainer, but if we never inquire of Him, how can we expect Him to teach us?

The fact is, the Holy Spirit wants to communicate with us on a frequent basis. Learning to communicate with the Holy Spirit is essential throughout our journey here on earth. The communication method generally happens through the Holy Spirit speaking to your spirit. When you receive Christ, the connection is made between your spirit and His, which becomes a Christian's most significant resource. You can now get clear direction from God for your life. The more you interact with the Holy Spirit, the more familiar you become with His voice and guidance. The Holy Spirit, the Word, and God the Father are all always unified. As a result of the Triune agreement, the Holy Spirit will never instruct you to do anything or say anything contrary to the written Word of God. A good trainer has

his student's best interest in mind and would correct any mistakes he sees them making. Like a trainer, the Holy Spirit is constantly coaching us and making us better followers of Christ. There have been times when I've said something wrong to someone, and before I get the words out, my spirit is checked. That is the time to correct the problem, repent, and learn from the mistake. The Holy Spirit knows the exact, perfect will for your life and will always lead you toward it!

Reading Study Questions

1. Explain a time when you served in a leadership role.

_____

_____

_____

_____

_____

2. What was your style of leading?

_____

_____

_____

_____

_____

3. What role does the Holy Spirit play in a believer's life?

_____

_____

_____

_____

_____

4. When you need direction, where do you go?

_____

_____

_____

_____

5. How does the Holy Spirit communicate?

_____

_____

_____

_____

6. Describe the feeling you experience when you are disobedient to the guidance of the Holy Spirit.

_____

_____

_____

_____

7. Explain some practices that will help you hear the Holy Spirit.

_____

_____

_____

_____

8. Will the Holy Spirit ever give direction that isn't in alignment with the written Word? Why?

_____

_____

_____

_____

_____

OUR PROVISION

CHAPTER 19: LOVE IN ACTION

Bible Study Verses: John 21:15–17, Acts 20:34–36
Memory Verse:

Dear children, let us not love with words or speech but with actions and in truth. (1 John 3:18 NIV)

Background

Love is expressed in a variety of different ways. In this chapter, you will discover God's view on love and what it means to love our neighbor.

Memory Verse Questions

1. Describe different ways you use the word *love*.

   _____

   _____

   _____

2. What does it mean to love with words or speech?

   _____

   _____

   _____

3. Explain what loving with action looks like.

   _____

   _____

   _____

4. Why is loving with action more important than loving with words or speech?

_____

_____

_____

5. Loving in truth is loving without pretense. Why do you think John included this method?

_____

_____

_____

6. Give an example of someone loving you this way. Describe the impact it made on you.

_____

_____

_____

Bible Study Questions: John 21:15–17, Acts 20:34–36

1. What is the Greek word Jesus used for *love* in John 21:15?

_____

_____

_____

_____

_____

2. What is the Greek word Peter used for *love* in his reply?

_____

_____

_____

_____

_____

3. What is the definition of the Greek word *agapao*?

    _____

    _____

    _____

    _____

    _____

4. What is the definition of the Greek word *phileo*?

    _____

    _____

    _____

    _____

    _____

5. Why do you think Peter answered using the word *phileo* instead of *agapao*?

    _____

    _____

    _____

    _____

    _____

6. Why was loving Jesus a prerequisite to feeding His sheep?

    _____

    _____

    _____

    _____

    _____

7. In Acts 20:35, we read that it's more blessed to give than receive. Explain why this is true.

_____

_____

_____

_____

_____

8. Share a time with your group where you experienced someone blessing you through giving.

_____

_____

_____

_____

_____

Words from the Author

Someone says, "I love God, but I don't care for the Church." This is like someone saying to me, "I love you, Pacer, but I don't care for your wife." I'm pretty sure I would take offense to that statement because Connie and I are one. When we develop a deep love for God, it will extend to His Bride and all of His children as well. As followers of Christ, we are instructed to love everyone, including our enemies. Jesus said that if you love God and love your neighbor, all the other commands hang on these two. I've often wondered why God would use these two simple actions to sum up all the required instructions found in the Law that Moses gave to the Israelites. The scripture tells us that God is love, which is evident by Him giving His Son for all humanity, including those who hated Him. I've noticed it's not that difficult to love my family or close friends, but what about the person at work whom I don't get along with, or the neighbor that causes problems? What about that person who intentionally did me wrong? Is God really asking, or should I say *commanding*, me to love them as well? The answer is yes. What seems to be two simple acts of love has now become somewhat difficult because before I can love my enemy, first I must forgive them. Jesus said in Matthew 5:46 that there's no reward for loving those who love you; even the tax collectors are doing that.

I've discovered that love is the most incredible evangelism tool we possess. Love in action opens the door to even the hardest of hearts. In 2007, our Church met in a local high school and prayed about leading

a community outreach event. We named the outreach Helping Hands, predicated around helping less-fortunate children with back-to-school supplies. What started as a simple act of love was now gaining momentum. Not only did the members of Revolution Church get excited about helping these children, but people in the community did as well. The first Helping Hands was a phenomenal success, with several hundred kids receiving school supplies, new shoes, clothes, haircuts, and much more. As a church, we've recognized that the more we love people, the more excellent the opportunity for sharing the message. This event is now ten years going and has grown from a few hundred to over seven thousand. Hundreds of people have decided to follow Christ due to this simple act of love. Expressing our love through giving builds a bridge to the heart.

Local outreach at Heritage High School in Maryville, TN.

At last year's event, a young single mother named Chasity with three children came to receive shoes and school supplies. Chasity's son received a new pair of shoes, but her two little girls didn't because we didn't have sizes that small. She was instructed to come by the Church Sunday morning before service and pick up a shoe gift card for her girls. That Sunday, she picked up her cards, but decided to stay for the early service. As a result of showing love to this single mom, she has accepted Jesus as Lord and Savior along with her son. She has been baptized and continues bringing

friends every Sunday! The last count I've heard, nine friends and family have received Christ and been baptized due to love in action. Not only are recipients touched by acts of love, but the ones who give are also blessed.

Paul referred to Jesus as saying, "It's more blessed to give than receive." At one of our previous Helping Hands events, I had a lady who was a member of our Church come up to me, very excited that her husband, Ricky, had come to serve. One of the reasons for the excitement was that her husband didn't attend Church, and this was his first church function. We asked him if he would be interested in helping the parking team, which he gladly accepted. I'll never forget how hot it was on that particular day as temps were in the upper nineties. The parking team had to be one of the most challenging jobs that day. The next day, Sunday, I was in the church foyer, and to my surprise, Ricky came walking into our Church for the first time and has never stopped coming. What's interesting about Ricky is his opportunity to serve became the catalyst for his conversion. In John 13:35, Jesus said, "Everyone would know you're My disciples if you love one another." Love in action works miracles!

Reading Study Questions

1. What are the two greatest commandments?

   _____

   _____

   _____

   _____

   _____

2. Is it possible to love God and not people? Explain.

   _____

   _____

   _____

   _____

   _____

3. Describe why it's difficult to love our enemies.

_____

_____

_____

_____

4. Why would God expect us to love everyone?

_____

_____

_____

_____

5. Why do you think love is an excellent evangelism tool?

_____

_____

_____

_____

6. Have you ever been in need, and someone showed you love in action? Share your story.

_____

_____

_____

_____

7. Why are so many people reluctant to attend Church? What can we do to remove the barriers?

_____

_____

_____

_____

_____

8. What are the greatest needs in your community? What can you do to help?

_____

_____

_____

_____

_____

CHAPTER 20: THE LEAST OF THESE

Bible Study Verses: Luke 10:25–37
Memory Verse:

> When he saw the crowds, he had compassion on them, because they were harassed and helpless, like sheep without a shepherd. (Matthew 9:36 NIV)

Background

Jesus not only preached the gospel, but lived it out in His community. In this chapter, we'll see how Jesus didn't shy away from interaction with the prostitute, lepers, or tax collectors, but made it a priority to minister to them.

Memory Verse Questions

1. What is your definition of *compassion*?

   _____

   _____

   _____

2. How do you respond when you're moved with compassion?

   _____

   _____

   _____

3. How did Jesus respond to the destitute people?

   _____

   _____

   _____

4. As Jesus was moved with compassion, he would heal the sick. What message did this send to His disciples? What message does this send to you?

_____

_____

_____

5. When you help someone who's helpless, what impact do you think it has on them? What effect would it have on you?

_____

_____

_____

6. If Jesus lived on earth today, what social issues would He be addressing?

_____

_____

_____

"Not all of us can do great things. But we can do small things with great love."

—Mother Teresa—

Bible Study Questions:
Luke 10:25–37

1. What was the question the expert in the law asked Jesus?

_____

_____

_____

_____

_____

2. What was his reasoning behind asking, "Who is my neighbor"?

_____

_____

_____

_____

_____

3. Why do you suppose the priest and Levite didn't stop to help the man in need?

_____

_____

_____

_____

_____

4. Why did the Samaritan stop to help?

_____

_____

_____

_____

_____

5. What can we learn from the Good Samaritan, and what actions can we take to be better neighbors?

_____

_____

_____

_____

_____

Words from the Author

The Good Samaritan can be seen as an antiquated story trenched in Hebrew culture, or can be viewed as a timeless tendency to overlook people in need. The simple act of being a good neighbor is a foundational principle that Christ emphasized. We can learn from this story that the lawyer asked a rhetorical question when he said, "What shall I do to inherit eternal life?" He knew what the law said and even gave Jesus the answer. Notice that Jesus referenced a priest and Levite as He shared the story that both men would have been very familiar with the law.

In modern-day society, it's viewed as the government's responsibility to care for the needs of the poor, widows, and orphans, which is in contrast with the teaching of Jesus. In the Good Samaritan case, two people missed an opportunity to help someone in dire need before the Samaritan arrived on the scene. Like the priest and Levite, we are so preoccupied with where we need to be next or our busy schedule that we walk past those who need us most.

I was recently made aware of a neighboring community's hunger issue in Monroe County. It was brought to my attention that three out of five children in this community go to bed hungry every night. After hearing this, I met with the principal of an elementary school in Monroe County to verify this information. He assured me of the problem, saying that kids come to school every day hungry. With permission from the school, we decided to place a food pantry where parents or kids could pick up food anytime school was in session. What was amazing was that food started streaming in and flowing out as soon as the pantry was built! Amazingly, the shelves have never been empty. I've discovered that when you prioritize the least of these, God supplies the resources to meet their needs.

The year 2020 presented lots of opportunities to reach out and assist people in need. No one could have predicted a global pandemic of the magnitude of COVID-19. Hospitals filled to maximum capacity, grocery stores with no food, and people without work. Restaurants, businesses, churches, and schools were all shut down. One of our church members, Steve Hepperly, had the idea of doing a weekly food distribution to meet the needs of our school-age children who were accustomed to having hot meals each day during school. Since the pandemic had shut down the schools, the concern was that many children wouldn't have adequate food. Now that our church services had gone entirely online, we had an eleven-hundred-seat sanctuary that could be converted to a food distribution center. Volunteers would come and box up food as the Church began purchasing pallets of food from warehouses in the region. The Church hired the local bus drivers to pick up and deliver the food each Wednesday morning. Principals, teachers, and volunteers would ride the bus routes and hand deliver the boxes to the children's door. The testimonies from this are extraordinary! A very dark time in world history has also been an opportune time to serve the least of these.

Reading Study Questions

1. Why do you think Jesus placed such emphasis on serving the least of these?

   _____

   _____

   _____

   _____

   _____

2. Do you find yourself drawn to the needs of people around you? Explain.

   _____

   _____

   _____

   _____

   _____

3. Whose responsibility is it to help the needy and poor?

   _____

   _____

   _____

   _____

   _____

4. How do you share the gospel of Jesus when helping someone in need?

   _____

   _____

   _____

   _____

   _____

5. During the pandemic, when many school children were without hot meals, whose responsibility was it for the children to be fed?

_____

_____

_____

_____

_____

6. If we wait on someone else to meet the needs, what could be the consequences?

_____

_____

_____

_____

_____

CHAPTER 21: PRINCIPLE OF GIVING

Bible Study Verses: Malachi 3:8–12, 2 Corinthians 9:6–15
Memory Verse:

Give, and it will be given to you: good measure, pressed down, shaken together, and running over will be put into your bosom. For with the same measure that you use, it will be measured back to you. (Luke 6:38 (NKJV)

Background:

When God gave His Son, He gave His very best because of His love for you. In this chapter, you will discover the joy and purpose of giving and the promises God has in store for the giver.

Memory Verse Questions

1. We can see throughout Scripture that giving precedes receiving. Why do you think this is so?

   _____

   _____

   _____

2. Which do you feel is easier, giving or receiving? Explain.

   _____

   _____

   _____

3. Does the amount you receive have any correlation to what you give?

   _____

   _____

   _____

4. Why do you feel some people are reluctant to give?

_____

_____

_____

5. Write a short testimony of when you've seen this giving/receiving principle in your life.

_____

_____

_____

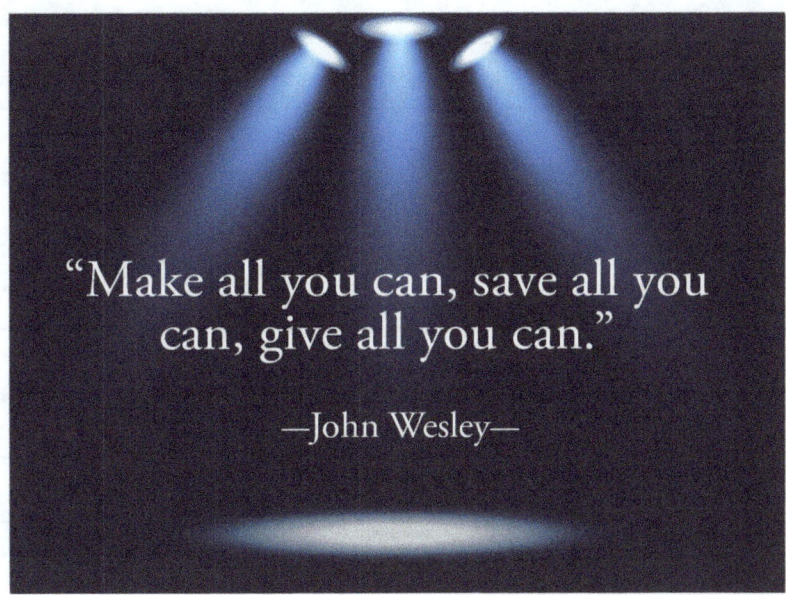

"Make all you can, save all you can, give all you can."

—John Wesley—

Bible Study Questions

1. In what way was Israel robbing God?

_____

_____

_____

_____

_____

2. What was the impact of their disobedience?

_____

_____

_____

_____

_____

3. Where did God require the tithe to be brought?

_____

_____

_____

_____

_____

4. What was the impact of their obedience?

_____

_____

_____

_____

_____

5. Explain what "rebuking the devourer" means.

_____

_____

_____

_____

_____

6. Share a testimony where God has blessed you for your obedience in giving.

_____

_____

_____

_____

_____

Words from the Author

I find it interesting that Jesus spent more time talking about money than He did about heaven and hell. Could it be Jesus understood that giving reflects the condition of the heart, and those who didn't give had a heart issue? That's heavy but true. Proverbs 4:23 tells us that everything flows from the heart. Think about it: every word and every action originates in the heart. Only a generous heart would cause a family to suspend a vacation and give to a needy family. Only a generous heart would cause a person to curb their appetite and give to a need in the Church. As I mentioned in chapter twenty, during the pandemic of 2020, the Church stepped up and began a food drive to alleviate hunger in our community.

Several things were happening simultaneously; all in-person services were suspended, while at the same time, we were spending lots of money to feed our community. Approximately five weeks passed before I realized the magnitude of this food drive. I was speaking with our finance department and asked for a summary of how much money we had spent on the food drive. To my surprise, I was given the total amount, over $93,000 had been spent on food and bus driver's transportation costs! I'm pretty sure my heart skipped a beat as this was a shock considering the food drive was not over yet!

At this point, I'm pretty sure I had more questions than answers. I wasn't sure if our church members would continue giving and tithing now that the state had mandated that no one could have in-person church services. What was amazing is that the Church didn't slow down their generosity, but the contributions increased! I remember receiving a call from a friend of mine during this time. He was calling to check on my family and the Church. In our phone conversation, he asked what the needs of the Church were. I responded that we continue to pay our full-time staff, which was twenty-two employees and six teachers in our mother's day out program, even though they couldn't work. I also let him know that we were feeding the children in our community.

Again, he asked a straightforward question. "What do you need?" I realized he was asking for a dollar amount, which I told him I didn't feel comfortable giving. Again, the third time he asked, "How much do you need?" Before I realized it, the number $100,000 just came out of my mouth. It got quiet for a second, which seemed like minutes. He then responded, "I can get you $30,000. Give me an hour, and I'll be there."

An hour passed, then two, and I was wondering if he was coming; then my phone rang. He said it took him a little while to rearrange his funds, but he was on his way not with $30,000, but a $100,000 check! Every dollar spent on food and transportation was replenished. The generosity of this individual allowed the Church to bless our community and not miss a beat. God taught me an incredible lesson that you can't out-give Him and that people will give to the Church when they realize it's going to be spent on needs and not just saved for the future.

Tithing is a foundational principle that goes so much deeper than money. It's giving your first fruits, not what's left over at the end of the week. I heard a statistic that if every church member tithes, we could completely eliminate world hunger. The first time tithe is mentioned in God's Word is in Genesis 14. Abraham was on his return from rescuing his nephew Lot when he encountered Melchizedek, the high priest. Abraham voluntarily offered him a tithe (tenth) of everything he owned. The word tithe means tenth and is found twenty-eight more times in the Old Testament. It appears twice in the New Testament, referring to Abraham's relationship to Christ by comparing Abraham's tithe and his acknowledgment of God. God explains in Malachi chapter three that God's blessing is attached to the tithe. He made it clear that He would open the windows and pour out blessings that cannot be contained!

Some people get confused with the tithe and offerings. The tithe is the first fruit that should be brought to the Church (storehouse), whereas the offering is left to our discretion and can be directed where we feel the Holy Spirit leading us. God has attached several promises to those who are obedient with the tithe. He said the devourer would be rebuked for a tither's sake and that all the world would call them blessed.

Malachi was given a word for Israel to return to God, and He would return to them. Israel had not only turned from God but had turned from His ordinances. Malachi 3:8: God asks this question, "Will a man rob God?" He continued by saying that they had robbed Him in tithes and offerings. This was such an offense to God that He cursed the entire nation. God made it clear that He would turn the curse into a blessing if Israel would be obedient with their tithe. The fact that God would put His reputation on the line for the tither is simply astonishing! He emphatically promised that the windows of heaven would be opened to the tither, along with blessings that we cannot contain. God said the devourer would be rebuked on behalf of the tither, and all nations would call you blessed! Some may ask the question of why a nonmaterialistic God would place so much emphasis on tithing and giving. The reason is that giving reflects the condition of the heart, and God's focus is on our hearts. The verse below reveals that God desires a cheerful heart because a cheerful heart is a generous heart.

Each of you should give what you have decided in your heart to give, not reluctantly or under compulsion, for God loves a cheerful giver. (2 Corinthians 9:7)

Reading Study Questions

1. Why do you think Jesus spent so much time discussing money and giving?

   _____

   _____

   _____

   _____

   _____

2. How does giving reflect the condition of the heart?

   _____

   _____

   _____

   _____

   _____

3. Have you ever had someone give you money when you were in need? Share your story.

   _____

   _____

   _____

   _____

   _____

4. Have you ever been compelled to give someone money and did or didn't? Explain.

   _____

   _____

   _____

   _____

   _____

5. Why is it important to bring our tithe to the Church?

_____

_____

_____

_____

_____

6. The tithe is intended for your Church (storehouse) so that there will be meat resources) in the house. Why do you think God included giving offerings?

_____

_____

_____

_____

_____

7. Have you experienced a time when you were generous, and God gave a blessing in return? Explain.

_____

_____

_____

_____

_____

CHAPTER 22: STEWARDSHIP

Bible Study Verses: Matthew 25:14–26
Memory Verse:

> His Lord said to him, "Well done, good and faithful servant; you were faithful over a few things, I will make you ruler over many things. Enter into the joy of your Lord." (Matthew 25:21 NKJV)

Background

When God completed the creation process, He entrusted Adam with stewarding what God had given him. Each of us has been entrusted to steward what God has given us. In this chapter, we will discover what stewardship looks like in our everyday life.

Memory Verse Questions

1. Write down three things that others would say you have done well.

   _____

   _____

   _____

2. How would you describe a good and faithful servant?

   _____

   _____

   _____

3. Name a few things you are to be faithful with.

   _____

   _____

   _____

4. Are there any areas in your life where you can improve your faithfulness? If so, list them.

_____

_____

_____

5. If the Lord gave you more responsibilities in His kingdom, how would you respond?

_____

_____

_____

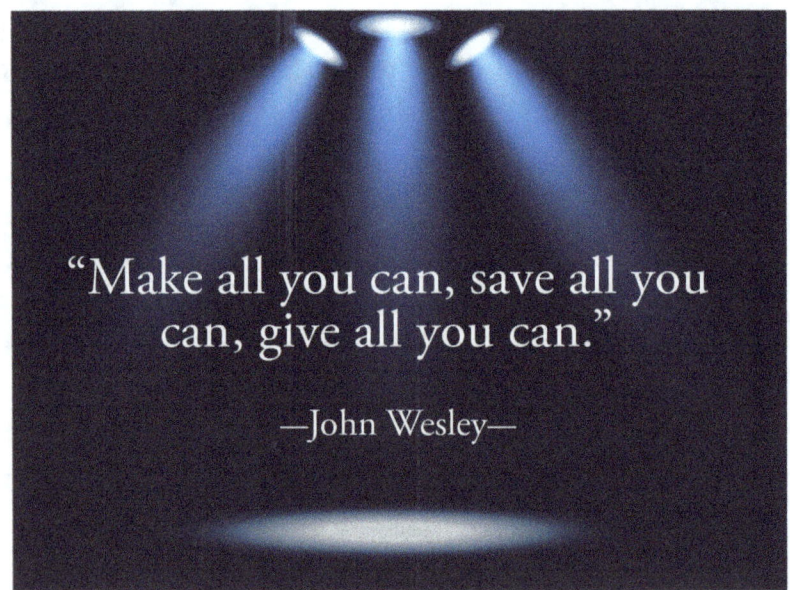

"Make all you can, save all you can, give all you can."

—John Wesley—

Bible Study Questions: Matthew 25:14–26

1. Name a few things that you have been responsible for managing.

_____

_____

_____

_____

_____

2. Do you see yourself as a five-talent, two-talent, or one-talent individual? Explain.

_____

_____

_____

_____

_____

3. Most people have a skewed personal view of their abilities. Have you struggled with low self-esteem? What does the Scripture teach us about our self-worth?

_____

_____

_____

_____

_____

Read Romans 8:37.

1. Explain how discipleship and stewardship are related.

_____

_____

_____

_____

2. What has God invested in you that He's expecting a return on?

_____

_____

_____

_____

_____

3. Why do you think the individual with one talent buried it? Have you ever buried a talent? If so, explain.

_____

_____

_____

_____

_____

4. Describe how the Lord responds to those who are good stewards with talents.

_____

_____

_____

_____

_____

5. Why do you think the Lord reacts harshly to the person who buries their talent?

_____

_____

_____

_____

_____

Words from the Author

I've often heard that God's not looking for our ability, but our availability. In this parable of the talents, God distributed them according to their ability. I find it quite interesting that the word *ability* is used here to determine the number of talents dispersed. What's even more interesting is that the original word from which ability is translated comes from the Greek word *dunamis*, meaning power for performing miracles, ability, strength. This is the same word that Jesus used in Acts 1:8 when He said, "You shall receive power (*dunamis*) when the Holy Spirit comes upon you." As we look deeper at this Greek word, we understand that the distribution of talents was not based on personal abilities, but reliance on the Holy Spirit.

As we learn to listen and take instructions from the Holy Spirit, we can see our

talents increase. This explains why the person that buried their talent was cast into outer darkness. It appears they didn't have the power (*dunamis*) of the Holy Spirit, or the ability to steward what God had given them. Romans 12:3 tells us that God has given everyone a measure of faith, but it's our responsibility to place that measure of faith in Jesus Christ which will translate into the ability to see the increase.

> For I say, through the grace given to me, to everyone who is among you, not to think of himself more highly than he ought to think, but to think soberly, as *God has dealt to each one a measure of faith.* (Romans 12:3 NKJV)

Considering that God is omniscient, He knows not only our ability, but also our readiness and willingness to disciple others. You have the ability not only to be a disciple of Jesus, but God has given you the power to disciple others as well. It all begins by activating that measure of faith and joining in a discipleship relationship with someone mature in their faith. As your faith matures through discipleship, you will eventually branch off and begin leading others. One of the reasons Christians never invest time in other people is because they feel inadequate. If Matthew, the tax collector, waited until he felt adequate, he would've never left his tax collector booth to follow Jesus. If Peter had waited until he was spiritually ready, he would've never left his family business to follow Jesus. Don't wait another minute if you have been procrastinating about stepping out and leading others. Take that step of faith and begin being a good steward of what God has invested in you. Few things bring more fulfillment than obedience to the call of Jesus and making disciples.

Pacer Hepperly recognizing his mentor Don Stephenson

One of the common questions you may ask is "how do I find someone to disciple?" I would strongly suggest that you begin by making it a point during your prayer time to ask God who you are to invest in. When the Holy Spirit shows you someone to disciple, go to them and have a conversation about discipleship. Share with them the commitment required to be a disciple of Christ. You will know pretty quickly if they are ready. The Holy Spirit has always given me confirmation on whether to move forward with someone or to continue praying for someone else. Over the years, I have discipled an incredibly diverse group of men, such as pastors, business leaders, and even new believers.

Currently, I have two men that I'm meeting with who have spent many years being incarcerated. Some may question, why invest in someone who has spent most of their life making bad decisions? Is that not a risky investment? Jesus selecting Matthew to disciple would seem chancy, considering his prior occupation was a tax collector in what most viewed as a dishonest trade. After Matthew spent several years with Jesus, he became an incredible disciple bearing much fruit proving the statement true *"to whom much is given much is required"* (Luke 12:48).

If Mr. Kimball, a Sunday school teacher, had not invested in the young man selling boots in his uncle's store, we may have never heard of the evangelist D. L. Moody, who reached millions for Christ.

If Mordecai Ham had not stewarded the gift God gave him, we might have never heard of Bill Graham, who impacted the world for Jesus.

I am incredibly blessed to have Don Stephenson as a mentor who has invested lots of time praying and mentoring me. Don is an incredible leader who has never pastored a church or authored a book. Still, he leads multiple discipleship groups of men who are lay members, businessmen, authors, and pastors of large congregations. You can influence multitudes simply by influencing one, which is what Don's doing. The next person God leads you to disciple could be a world changer for Jesus!

Reading Study Questions

1. Have you ever viewed yourself as an influencer? Explain.

   _____

   _____

   _____

   _____

   _____

2. Think about three people who have positively influenced you and share with the group how they have impacted you.

   _____

   _____

   _____

   _____

   _____

3. At this point in the book, you are ready to begin looking for someone to disciple. What are some of the feelings you have about discipleship?

_____

_____

_____

_____

_____

4. When approaching someone about discipleship, what are some of the questions you will ask them?

_____

_____

_____

_____

_____

5. How will you determine if someone is or is not a good candidate for your discipleship program?

_____

_____

_____

_____

_____

6. Why is it essential to give your discipleship student your best effort?

_____

_____

_____

_____

_____

7. Name some people from the Bible whom God selected for significant assignments that had a sketchy past.

_____

_____

_____

_____

_____

8. Explain how Mr. Kimball, the Sunday school teacher, reached millions of people.

_____

_____

_____

_____

_____

CHAPTER 23: PROVISION

Bible Study Verses: 1 Timothy 5:8, Ephesians 6:4, Joshua 24:15
Memory Verse:

> Train up a child in the way he should go, And when he is old he will not depart from it. (Proverbs 22:6 NKJV)

Background

Scripture teaches us that God is our ultimate provider. We also see that God greatly emphasizes parents providing for their household. A Godly Christian environment is the greatest thing you can provide for your family. A place where the Word of God is taught and Jesus is honored. This chapter gives excellent insight on how to begin discipleship in your home.

Memory Verse Questions

1. What is the promise our memory verse gives us?

   _____

   _____

   _____

2. Why is training necessary for our children?

   _____

   _____

   _____

3. Name a few ways that society intentionally or inadvertently influences our children.

   _____

   _____

   _____

4. Does parental training ever end? If no, give some examples.

_____

_____

_____

5. What training did you receive in your home as a child? Explain.

_____

_____

_____

6. Do you think public schools support what's taught in Christian homes? Explain.

_____

_____

_____

Bible Study Questions: 1 Timothy 5:8, Ephesians 6:4, Joshua 24:15

1. What does 1 Timothy 5:8 say about a believer who doesn't provide for their family?

_____

_____

_____

_____

_____

2. Name several ways that we should provide for our families.

_____

_____

_____

_____

_____

3. Explain how important it is to provide spiritual guidance to our family.

_____

_____

_____

_____

_____

4. In your own words, explain what it means not to provoke your children to wrath.

_____

_____

_____

_____

_____

5. What are some effective methods for training children?

_____

_____

_____

_____

_____

6. As the leader of your house, name some principles that you consider to be non-negotiables.

_____

_____

_____

_____

Words from the Author

I'll be the first to say raising children isn't an easy task. I have two sons, Joshua and Hunter, who are married and have their own children. Connie and I often told them, you will reap what you sow, and now having children, they are enjoying the harvest. I'm sure they are telling their children the same thing we told them. Connie and I learned through trial and error that just because you raise your children in Church doesn't mean that they will always do the right thing. Like every parent, we've faced some obstacles, but I'm very proud that both Josh and Hunter are actively involved in Church and are now raising their children in Church.

What's more impressive from my perspective is that they are teaching their children Godly principles in their homes. This is a great responsibility considering a child's first impression of God comes from the parents in many cases. Recently, at a family gathering, I was having a conversation with my sons about raising children in the world today and shared that I don't envy their job. We were talking about how society teaches so many things that are in opposition to biblical values. I asked them, "How do you guys deal with your children being exposed to all these anti-biblical views?" Josh shared that he teaches his children that nothing they hear supersedes what is taught in their home, which includes teachers, curriculum, internet, movies, etc. Providing an atmosphere in the home where children are

trained in the things of God is essential in their pursuit of God.

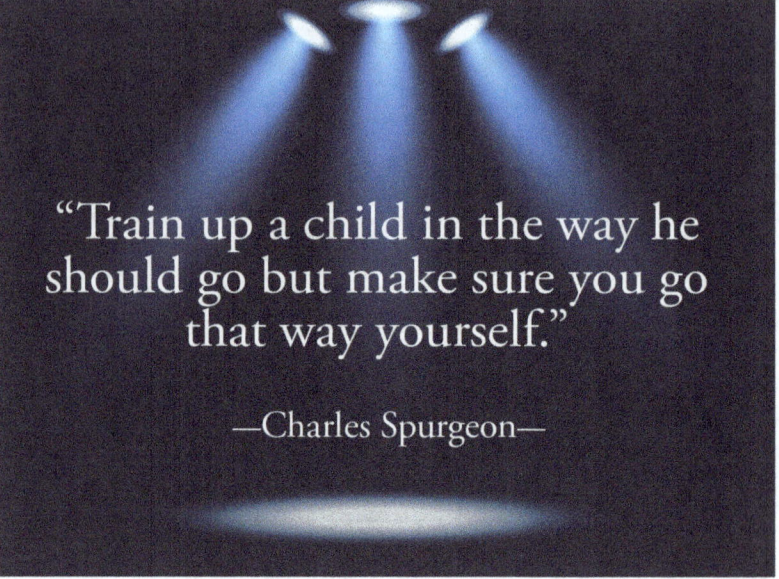

"Train up a child in the way he should go but make sure you go that way yourself."

—Charles Spurgeon—

Regarding children's discipleship, there's not one size fits all or a cookie-cutter model, but I've discovered several things that I've found helpful. I would suggest having a daily Bible devotion along with family prayer time. These times will prove to be instrumental in the spiritual growth of your children. Just as our Heavenly Father has provided everything we need to be successful in our Christian walk, we can do the same to ensure our children's success. If you're reading this book and didn't implement these processes with your family, don't beat yourself up; it's not too late to begin. Make a decision today that your home will be a place where God is honored, and discipleship is prioritized.

Joshua understood the value of providing Godly leadership in the home. Look at what he said.

And if it seems evil to you to serve the Lord, choose for yourselves this day whom you will serve, whether the gods which your fathers served that were on the other side of the River, or the gods of the Amorites, in whose land you dwell. But *as for me and my house, we will serve the Lord.* (Joshua 24:15 NKJV)

I find it intriguing that He spoke for his entire family: "As for me and my house, we will serve the Lord."

I initially thought that Joshua was referring to his immediate family when I read this. Still, as I look deeper into this passage, I realize he was also speaking on behalf of his extended family. Joshua's family respected him because he had invested in them. He had trained them in things of God, and he was confident that they wouldn't serve the gods of the Amorites. Training is accomplished in a variety of different ways.

1. *Joshua led by example.*
2. *He faced difficult situations with confidence that God would bring them through.*
3. *He was a positive role model.*
4. *He was an effective communicator.*
5. *He was a consistent leader.*

I find it interesting that Moses, Joshua's mentor, demonstrated all of these extraordinary characteristics that Joshua possessed. Joshua became the incredible leader he was because he was trained exceptionally well.

While raising boys, there were many times I questioned my parenting skills. As with many children, my sons ventured off the straight and narrow path, but thankfully there is great truth in our memory verse, "Train up a child in the way they should go, and when they are old they will not depart from it."

Reading Study Guide

1. Is raising children difficult? Explain.

_____

_____

_____

_____

_____

2. Why is it essential to teach Godly principles in the home?

    _____

    _____

    _____

    _____

    _____

3. Do you see anything that society promotes that contradicts God's Word? If so, name a few.

    _____

    _____

    _____

    _____

    _____

4. What are some spiritual practices that we can implement in our homes?

    _____

    _____

    _____

    _____

    _____

5. Name some good characteristics that Joshua possessed.

    _____

    _____

    _____

    _____

    _____

6. Where do you think Joshua acquired these characteristics?

_____

_____

_____

_____

_____

7. Name three things that God has given you that you can pass on to others.

_____

_____

_____

_____

_____

OUR CHURCH

CHAPTER 24: THE CHURCH

Bible Study Verses: 1 Corinthians 12:12–27, Colossians 1:18
Memory Verse:

> And I also say to you that you are Peter, and on this rock I will build My Church, and the gates of Hades shall not prevail against it. (Matthew 16:18 NKJV)

Background

The Church and Jesus are inseparable, considering Jesus is the head, and the Church is the Body. After Jesus's ascension, He established the Church and empowered it with authority to carry out His mission on earth.

Memory Verse questions

1. Who is the builder of the Church?

   _____

   _____

   _____

2. Jesus wasn't saying that He was building the Church on Peter, but on this rock; what is the rock Jesus was referring to?

   _____

   _____

   _____

3. What do you think this statement by Christ means: "The gates of Hades will not prevail against it."

   _____

   _____

   _____

4. Can you think of several ways Satan has tried to destroy the Church?

_____

_____

_____

5. List several ways the Church can be on the offensive and drive out darkness.

_____

_____

_____

Bible Study Questions: 1 Corinthians 12:12–27, Colossians 1:18

1. What analogy does Paul use to describe the Body of Christ?

_____

_____

_____

_____

_____

2. What body part is Jesus referred to as?

_____

_____

_____

_____

_____

3. Are there any body parts that aren't important?

_____

_____

_____

_____

_____

4. List some body parts we esteem higher than others, and list some that are viewed as less important.

_____

_____

_____

_____

_____

5. In verse 25, Paul says we should have equal concern for one another and that there be no division. Give some examples of how this can be accomplished in the Church.

_____

_____

_____

_____

_____

6. What body part would describe the role you play in the Church?

_____

_____

_____

_____

_____

Words from the Author

The word Church is first mentioned in Matthew 16:18 and is translated from the Greek word *ekklesia*. This word simply means "Called Out Assembly." As believers in Christ, we have been called out from this world and grafted into the Body of Christ. Matthew gave an account of Peter receiving a divine revelation of who Jesus was. He said, "You are Christ, the Son of the living God." Acknowledging Jesus as the Son of God and accepting Him as savior immediately places you in the Body of Christ. We become alive in Christ during this conversion process. The Church is a living organism with Jesus being the head who instructs

the body parts to carry out His mission on the earth.

It's important to understand that the Church is not a human institution run by certain denominations. When we observe the analogy Paul gives using human anatomy, we see that the Church is made up of not just Jews, but Gentiles as well. In today's terminology, Paul would say the Church is made up of Baptist, Methodist, Church of God, Non-Denomination, etc.

Recently I completed a twelve-week sermon series titled Until Unity. Francis Chan wrote an incredible book titled *Until Unity* which I used as a reference point for the series. As I spent time reading the book and studying unity, I found that I needed to do a much better job building unity with pastors in my local community. As the series ended, I mentioned to our congregation that I would love to see our local pastors come together and work in unity across our area. This idea sounded great, but seeing it actually happen would require a miracle from God.

Not long after the unity series, I discovered that Terry Wilson, one of our Church members, had been attending an ecumenical prayer meeting gathering weekly to pray for our community. Terry had spoken to me several times about his desire to have a community service that included different denominations. I honestly didn't think it would work because our churches are so territorial. To my surprise, this idea began to gain momentum in the prayer group, and a meeting was scheduled. Terry Wilson personally invited approximately two hundred local pastors to the meeting. Seeing more than fifty pastors and church leaders gather and strategize on how we could make a positive impact in our community for Christ was such a glorious sight. At that meeting, we collectively agreed on a foundational belief and mission statement of faith that we would all adhere to.

Here is an abbreviated version of what we all agreed on.

- *We believe in the one Triune God: Father, Son and Holy Spirit.*
- *We believe in the Son, Jesus Christ, the Eternal Word, Who is God made flesh, the Lord and Redeemer of all humanity in Whom alone is salvation, not by works of man, but by repentance toward God and faith in the Lord Jesus Christ.*
- *We believe in Holy Scripture as the unique, divinely inspired Word.*
- *We believe that God created the universe and everything in it.*
- *We believe that God created man, and that in doing so He created man in His image and both male and female.*

- *We believe that God instituted and ordained the family. Accordingly, marriage is a sacred covenant between one man and one woman.*
- *We believe that human sexuality is a gift from God and should be offered back to Him either in marriage for procreation and union, or in celibacy for undivided devotion to Christ.*
- *We believe that the family is the fundamental building block and institution of society.*
- *We believe that children are a gift and blessing from God.*

- *We believe in the sanctity of life, Human life must be protected and defended from conception to natural death.*
- *We believe that God requires us to love everyone.*
- *We believe that because we must love everyone, we must speak truth in love and with compassion, and not in a spirit of militancy or anger.*
- *We believe that religious freedom is the primary and fundamental freedom, and that our religious heritage must have a place in the public arena.*
- *We believe that we have the right to speak without persecution or discrimination. In accordance with the aforestated beliefs we, as an association, agree to be on mission to take action as follows:*
- *We refuse to allow politics, race, denomination, or any other non-essential divisive difference to separate or damage our Kingdom Unity.*

As a result of our faith-based community coming together and identifying what we all agree on, this allowed us to take the next step and have a community revival. The revival began on January 1, 2022, and lasted twenty-one days. The agreed-upon structure was that each Church involved would open its pulpit up to allow a pastor from another church to preach during the revival. The twenty-one-day revival was an astounding success. Each night the services were packed full! Some nights there was standing room only. As the word spread throughout the community, more churches came on board. The continued growth of the revival required us to expand the meetings to multiple locations on the same night. When the twenty-one-day community revival ended, people began to ask when we will do this again. We now have future community revivals scheduled, with more churches added to the event. Incredible relationships have been built within our faith community due to focusing on what we agree on, not our differences.

Paul emphasized that the Body is made up of many parts and all parts are of equal value. In the Church, we often place a higher value on specific positions, leading to envy or jealousy. When this happens, it tends to elevate some while devaluing others. Paul used the analogy of the eye saying to the hand; I don't need you when all body parts are essential for overall success. In reality, none of the body parts are self-sufficient, but all rely on others to be complete. Psalm 133 declares where brethren dwell together in unity there, God commands the blessing, which is the place I want to be. It's in this unity where the Church thrives. It's in this unity that lost people are drawn to Christ. It's in this unity where the Church functions at total capacity!

The Church and Jesus are inseparable. It's impossible to function as an effective Christian without being actively part of the Church. One of Satan's tools he uses to pull Christians away from the Church comes through offenses. The Bible teaches that Satan is the accuser of the brethren, which means he's constantly making false accusations against brothers and sisters in Christ. By understanding his tactics, you can avoid the traps he's continually setting. We know that the Church is not made up of perfect people, but those whom the blood of Jesus has redeemed. Christ is the only one perfect, and that's why His position is the head.

As a believer, the Church has been vital in my spiritual growth. As a husband, the Church has helped me become a better leader for my family. As a father, it has helped me raise my children. As a pastor, it has helped me see value in every member.

Reading Study Guide

1. What is the Greek word for Church? What is its meaning?

   _____

   _____

   _____

   _____

   _____

2. How do you become part of the Church?

   _____

   _____

   _____

   _____

   _____

3. What is the purpose of the Church?

   _____

   _____

   _____

   _____

   _____

4. Explain what you think Paul meant when he said, "We are one body whether Jew or Gentiles, slave or free."

_____

_____

_____

_____

_____

5. Why do you think God places so much emphasis on unity in the Body of Christ?

_____

_____

_____

_____

_____

6. Why is it not a good idea to elevate certain positions in the Church above others?

"Every believer is commanded to be plugged in to a local church."

—David Jeremiah—

_____

_____

_____

_____

_____

7. Why are offenses in the Body of Christ dangerous?

_____

_____

_____

_____

_____

8. Share how the Church has been a benefit to you during your spiritual journey.

_____

_____

_____

_____

_____

CHAPTER 25: GIFTS

Bible Study Verses: Romans 12:3–8, 1 Corinthians 12:4–11, Ephesians 4:11–16
Memory Verse:

> Every good gift and every perfect gift is from above, and comes down from the Father of lights, with whom there is no variation or shadow of turning. (James 1:17 NKJV)

Background

Christ has generously distributed gifts throughout the Body of Christ to edify the Church. There is a fantastic fulfillment when you discover your gifts and begin utilizing them in the Church.

Memory Verse Questions

1. According to the memory verse, who distributes gifts?

   _____

   _____

   _____

2. Name some gifts you would best describe as good and perfect.

   _____

   _____

   _____

3. Why do you think God wants His children to have good gifts?

   _____

   _____

   _____

4. Explain a time when you gave someone a good gift and how it made you feel.

_____

_____

_____

5. Explain a time when someone gave you a gift that brought you joy.

_____

_____

_____

Bible Study Questions: Romans 12:3–8, 1 Corinthians 12:4–11, Ephesians 4:11–16

1. In Romans 12:3, how does Paul say we are to view ourselves?

_____

_____

_____

_____

_____

2. Why do you think our gifts are different in the Body of Christ?

_____

_____

_____

_____

_____

3. List the gifts that Paul mentions in Romans 12:6–8.

_____

_____

_____

_____

_____

4. List the gifts that Paul mentions in 1 Corinthians 12:8–10 and explain how each gift would be beneficial to the Church.

_____

_____

_____

_____

_____

5. List the five ministry gifts Paul mentions in Ephesians 4:11.

_____

_____

_____

_____

_____

6. According to Ephesians 4:12, what can we expect to see in the Body of Christ when these gifts are at work?

_____

_____

_____

_____

_____

7. Paul explains that maturity and unity will accompany the manifestation of these gifts; according to verse 14, name three things we can expect when they are not in operation.

_____

_____

_____

_____

_____

Words from the Author

Where does your mind go when you think of gifted individuals? Loving sports, I often think of great athletes such as Peyton Manning and Tom Brady, two of the greatest quarterbacks ever. Tiger Woods, in his prime, was dominant on the PGA Tour, making 142 consecutive cuts, crushing the previous record of 113. When you think of gifted individuals, maybe Elon Musk comes to mind as the founder of Tesla and SpaceX, along with many other companies.

"As God's children, we are not to be observers; we're to participate actively in the Lord's work. Spectators sit and watch, but we are called to use our spiritual gifts and serve continually."

—Charles Stanley—

Regardless of who comes to mind, one thing is for sure: some people have been given extraordinary gifts. I'd like to make a profound statement and say that everyone has been given incredible gifts. Our memory verse in this chapter explains that every good and perfect gift is from God. Could you imagine what a better world we would live in if everyone acknowledged God with their gifts and used them to edify the Body of Christ? I have two brothers and a sister that are very gifted and use their talents in the Body of Christ.

My oldest brother has an incredible gift of leadership. One of his first leading roles in the Church was serving as a volunteer youth pastor. During this time, the ministry experienced unprecedented growth. Later he would become a lead pastor and again experience extraordinary growth. To date, he has helped plant hundreds of churches and oversees an enormous mission project in Southeast Asia.

My sister has also been gifted with ministry gifts. She and her husband have pastored for several years and have served their Churches incredibly well. Her love for the congregation is an undeniable gift God has given her. Her love for her family is an extension of the ministry gift the Lord has blessed her with.

My younger brother and his wife have a supernatural gift of giving. God has used him and his wife to build church buildings, fund mission programs, and care for the hurting and poor. They have multiple businesses that absolutely thrive because they understand that the gift is from God and will be used to fund the Kingdom and edify the Church. As I'm writing now, I'm sitting in one of his properties in Florida where he and his wife graciously offered a quiet place to complete this book.

Imagine the impact the Church would have if most believers identified their God-given gifts and began using them to strengthen the Body of Christ. I am convinced that everything the Church needs to operate efficiently has been placed within the local body of believers. Two necessary things are identification and affirmation of these gifts. I wonder how many people sit in our churches with amazing God-given gifts but don't realize it. If you're reading this book and are unsure what your gift/gifts are, begin praying and asking God to reveal them to you. Talk with your spiritual leaders and get their input. As you discover your gift, start developing it! Like all the gifted individuals I previously mentioned, they all spent time cultivating their gifts. I'm pretty sure Peyton Manning didn't become a hall-of-fame quarterback without an incredible amount of coaching and intense training. If you put in the effort, God will see that your gift has a place to be used, and it will bring incredible fulfillment to your life!

When someone acknowledges a gift in your life, it builds your faith and allows you to begin developing the gift. Do you think Gideon would have defeated the Midianites if the angel hadn't acknowledged his gifts? Gideon saw himself as a coward, while God saw him as a warrior. It was initially hard to comprehend when the angel spoke and called him a mighty man of valor, but this positive affirmation would prove true.

Several years ago, my boss and I worked at a charity event before I was pastoring. While talking with people at the event, my boss commented that I was an excellent communicator. I had never viewed myself that way, being a natural introvert, but his words spoke volumes and gave me a massive boost of encouragement. A positive comment gave me faith and courage that God wanted me to develop this gift. I've discovered that if we humbly ask God to use us for the edifying of the Church, He will do exceedingly abundantly above what we could ask or think. When my boss paid me that compliment, I was a children's pastor speaking to a small number of children each Sunday. A few years later, God would have me communicating with several thousand people each weekend.

Whether speaking to thousands or speaking to one, your gift is essential to the health of the Church. Several years back, a man, Jim Reno, in our Church was gifted in intercessory prayer. A young couple in our Church had been trying to have children for several years without success. I recall Jim coming to me at the end of a service and sharing that he felt led to pray for this cou-

ple and ask my thoughts. I said absolutely, let's pray over them. We gathered around them, and Jim began to pray rather quietly. There was no lighting from heaven, no earthquake—just a simple, humble prayer. After praying, everyone respectively left the service.

A few weeks passed, and I received a phone call from the young man we had prayed over. He was excited to tell me that his wife had taken a pregnancy test and tested positive! Nine months later, they had a beautiful little girl named Sarah. I witnessed a miracle, and God had gifted this humble layman in our Church with the gift of faith. Over the years before Jim went to be with Jesus, I witnessed him pray over several couples who miraculously gave birth to children. There's not an all-inclusive list of gifts in the Bible, but several are mentioned. Seek after your gift, and when you discover it, cultivate it and use it for the glory of God.

Reading Study Guide

1. When you hear the word gifted, what comes to your mind?

   _____

   _____

   _____

   _____

   _____

2. List several people who are close to you and share what gifts you see in them.

   _____

   _____

   _____

   _____

   _____

3. This is a group exercise. Make a list of the people going through this book with you and write down the gifts you see in their life. Take turn about sharing the results.

   _____

   _____

   _____

_____

_____

4. What did the angel see in Gideon that he couldn't see?

_____

_____

_____

_____

_____

5. Why do you think we strug-
    gle to see our gifts?

_____

_____

_____

_____

"When you find your spiritual gift, God will give you an opportunity to use it."

—John C. Maxwell—

_____

6. What gift do you think God wants to use in your life to edify the Church?

_____

_____

_____

_____

_____

7. What can you do to cultivate this gift?

_____

_____

_____

_____

_____

CHAPTER 26: SPIRITUAL WARFARE

Bible Study Verses: 2 Kings 6:11–17, Daniel 10:7–13, Galatians 5:16–17, Matthew 4:1–11

Memory Verse:

> For we do not wrestle against flesh and blood, but against principalities, against powers, against the rulers of the darkness of this age, against spiritual hosts of wickedness in the heavenly places. (Ephesians 6:12 NKJV)

Background

There's a constant ploy in the dark unseen realm to undermine God's plan. This conflict is known as spiritual warfare and has been around since the fall of Satan. To better understand this phenomenon, we will delve deep into the Word and discover the role we are to play.

Memory Verse Questions

1. Give an example of wrestling against flesh and blood.

   _____

   _____

   _____

2. Name some ways the enemy causes fights between fellow believers.

   _____

   _____

   _____

3. How often do you think demons instigate arguments or disagreements between brothers and sisters?

   _____

   _____

   _____

4. Is it intimidating to know that you are battling against demons or fallen angels? Explain.

_____

_____

_____

5. Do you feel we must understand the tactics of our enemy? Why?

_____

_____

_____

"I believe that the attacks on your life have much more to do with who you might be in the future than who you have been in the past."

—Lisa Bevere—

Bible Study Questions: 2 Kings 6:11–17, Daniel 10:7–13, Galatians 5:16–17, Matthew 4:1–11

1. In 2 Kings 6:15, what caused Elisha's servant to worry and fear?

_____

_____

_____

_____

_____

2. Explain Elisha's response to his servant.

_____

_____

_____

_____

_____

3. How would we respond differently to unpleasant situations if our eyes were open to the unseen realm?

_____

_____

_____

_____

_____

4. Daniel 10:7–13: Explain what caused Daniel's prayer to be delayed.

_____

_____

_____

_____

_____

5. According to Galatians 5:16–17, what does this battle consist of?

_____

_____

_____

_____

_____

6. How can we be assured of a victory?

_____

_____

_____

_____

_____

7. How did Jesus prepare for spiritual warfare in the wilderness?

_____

_____

_____

_____

8. How did Jesus respond to Satan's temptation? What can you learn from this?

_____

_____

_____

_____

_____

Words from the Author

When we hear of war and fighting, it usually has a negative connotation, and rightfully so. A war indicates that at least two parties are battling for something they deem valuable. Revelation 12:7–9 gives us a picture of the first battle in heaven.

> And war broke out in Heaven: Michael and his angels fought with the dragon; and the dragon and his angels fought, but they did not prevail, nor was a place found for them in Heaven any longer. So the great dragon was cast out, that serpent of old, called the Devil and Satan, who deceives the whole world; he was cast to the Earth, and his angels were cast out with him. (Revelation 12:7–9 NKJV)

Satan and the fallen angels being cast down to the earth was not the end of spiritual warfare, but the beginning. We see Satan and his demons scheming to undermine God's plan from the beginning of Genesis until his final demise. War, in many cases, can be avoided by constraining the aggressor. The most effective weapon believers possess is prayer. Prayer paralyzes the enemy and allows the Kingdom of God to advance. In warfare, there's always an objective that usually boils down to control and possession. Realizing this explains why Satan has targeted the Church. He realizes the Church is God's possession, and Jesus established it to further His Kingdom. He also understands that if the Church is crippled, the Kingdom is weakened, and then he can push his agenda on the earth. As we have previously determined, the Church is not a building or denomination, but it's the called-out ones who gather as the Body of Christ. As believers, we understand that the battle is real even though we usually can't see it with our natural eyes. We must see ourselves as victors, not victims, which becomes obvious, understanding Jesus has already won the battle! Yes, I need to say that again, *Jesus has already won the battle!*

In the last two years, I have recognized spiritual warfare has increased, and the battle has intensified against the Church. Throughout the global pandemic, all-out war was unleashed on the Church. It began with officials passing laws prohibiting gatherings. These laws may have appeared to be caring and innocent from the public's perspective, but in reality, it was an attack orchestrated by principalities and wickedness in high places. This strategic move caused separation and isolation, which in turn had a nasty effect on the Church and society. Suicide began to skyrocket at unprecedented rates. Divorce increased at unprecedented numbers. The Church's only way of communicating with its body was through video streaming. Easter 2020, churches were not allowed to meet legally.

Some pastors who continued to gather were put in jail. As with any military operation, Satan had a plan, and it would begin by isolating the Body of Christ. Soon after the isolation came the propaganda designed to create division among the believers. Not long after the Churches stopped meeting, I began to see division as I had never witnessed. Church members were arguing over the mask or no mask, vaccination or no vaccination, gatherings or no gatherings. It became apparent to me that the Church was under a severe attack. Many Churches closed while others struggled to keep their doors open. As the governing officials began to allow Churches to gather again, many believers didn't come back. I have heard numbers as high as 60 percent of church members wouldn't return to the House of God, while many Churches would close permanently. As mature disciples of Jesus, we shouldn't helplessly stand by and do nothing, but we should actively be involved in the fight against darkness. Prayer, fasting, and studying the Word are essential elements in overcoming darkness and can be reviewed in section 2 of this book, Foundations.

Three takeaways:

The evils of darkness cannot coexist where the gospel is preached, but will always succumb to its power.

Discipleship is the model Jesus used to build soldiers that have proven successful.

A Church without disciples is like an army without soldiers.

Reading Study Guide:

1. Describe the battle of Revelation 12:7–9.

   _____

   _____

   _____

   _____

   _____

2. What is one of the most effective weapons for spiritual warfare?

   _____

   _____

   _____

   _____

   _____

3. Why do you think the Church is a primary target for Satan?

   _____

   _____

   _____

   _____

   _____

4. List three things needed for spiritual warfare.

   _____

   _____

   _____

   _____

   _____

5. How does darkness respond to the gospel being preached?

_____

_____

_____

_____

6. What was the model Jesus used to prepare His men for the mission?

_____

_____

_____

_____

7. Have a testimonial time where each person shares with the group how discipleship has impacted their life.

_____

_____

_____

_____

As you have completed this book, I pray that you will live your life entirely devoted to Jesus, growing into the mature Christian He desires. I hope that you will take what you have learned and invest it in others, which is vital to continued discipleship.

Having a graduation ceremony for the participants where spouses are invited is highly recommended.

ACKNOWLEDGMENTS

Thank you to my brother, Ronnie, for encouragement and leadership in authoring Purposeful Discipleship.

Thank you to my brother, Steve, and his wife, Tina, for providing a place of refuge to reflect and write.

Don Stephenson, thank you for your mentorship and guidance over the years.

Stephanie Walker thank you for helping to make the vision of these pages come to life.

And to My Family
Josh, Codi, Barrett, Tirzah, Archer, Talia, Hunter, Stacey, Addison, Lydia & Everly thank
you for being patient and understanding during the time it took to write this book.

Special thanks to my wife Connie for your support, patience, and love as you have
always been my biggest cheerleader regardless of the task at hand.

ABOUT THE AUTHOR

 Pacer Hepperly is a renowned teacher/student on the subject of discipleship. He has a business background with a pastoral heart. He currently pastors a thriving church that began as a church plant with thirty-nine members in 2007 and now has several campuses ministering to thousands each weekend. Pacer attributes this phenomenal growth to simply following the discipleship model that Jesus has laid out in the scripture. He has spent the last decade intrinsically motivated to sharing this model of multiplication through discipleship not only with his congregation but throughout Africa, Chile, Argentina, and Mexico.

www.ingramcontent.com/pod-product-compliance
Lightning Source LLC
Chambersburg PA
CBHW080818120626
46556CB00010B/3331